Parenting
at Our Best

Andi,
Thank you for your wisdom and advice
Love Allison

Parenting
at Our Best

*Wisdom and Advice from Parents
Who Have Been There*

Allison Merkle Alison

Edited by Kristin Collis

BALBOA
PRESS
A DIVISION OF HAY HOUSE

Copyright © 2012 Allison Merkle Alison

All rights reserved. No part of this book may be used or reproduced by any means, graphic, electronic, or mechanical, including photocopying, recording, taping or by any information storage retrieval system without the written permission of the publisher except in the case of brief quotations embodied in critical articles and reviews.

ISBN: 978-1-4525-5937-7 (sc)
ISBN: 978-1-4525-5938-4 (e)
ISBN: 978-1-4525-5939-1 (hc)

Library of Congress Control number: 2012918062

Balboa Press books may be ordered through booksellers or by contacting:

Balboa Press
A Division of Hay House
1663 Liberty Drive
Bloomington, IN 47403
www.balboapress.com
1-(877) 407-4847

Because of the dynamic nature of the Internet, any web addresses or links contained in this book may have changed since publication and may no longer be valid. The views expressed in this work are solely those of the author and do not necessarily reflect the views of the publisher, and the publisher hereby disclaims any responsibility for them.

The author of this book does not dispense medical advice or prescribe the use of any technique as a form of treatment for physical, emotional, or medical problems without the advice of a physician, either directly or indirectly. The intent of the author is only to offer information of a general nature to help you in your quest for emotional and spiritual well-being. In the event you use any of the information in this book for yourself, which is your constitutional right, the author and the publisher assume no responsibility for your actions.

Any people depicted in stock imagery provided by Thinkstock are models, and such images are being used for illustrative purposes only.
Certain stock imagery © Thinkstock.

Printed in the United States of America

Balboa Press rev. date: 11/30/2012

Acknowledgments

My deepest thanks to:

All the parents who let me interview them and who opened up to me and shared their parental wisdom, stories, and authentic selves. The time I spent with you was a gift I will never forget. I learned so much from you and hope I have adequately passed on your insight.

Kristin Collis, my editor and friend. You are a gifted writer and teacher. Thank you for all your hard work and encouragement.

My parents, who loved me unconditionally and gave me a wonderful, happy upbringing. Your support and encouragement throughout my life has enabled me to be the person I am today.

My amazing husband, David. You bring out the best in me. Thank you for supporting me through all my many careers—attorney, teacher, and now author. You are a fantastic father, and I am so glad you are my partner.

My children, Jocelyn, Davey, and Julia. You are without a doubt the most amazing people, and I love being your mom. A special thanks to Sam for taking such good care of my daughter.

My siblings, Bernie, Jeanne, and Tommy, and their spouses, Suzanne, Gary, and Araceli (and ex, Linda), who created this magnificent family group for my children to be nurtured in. Special thanks to Jeanne and Gary for being my children's guardians. I always knew that no matter what happened to David and me, you would love them like your own.

My nieces and nephews Justin, Danny, Jimmy, Billy, Jackie, Joyce, John, Reagan, Will, Caroline, and new addition Jenny. It has been my privilege to be part of your lives. I enjoy all our family times together and look forward to many more.

My grandparents, who have passed on and who started this beautiful family full of love and support.

My in-laws, Dave and Lee, and my brother-in-law, Daryl, who treated me like their own daughter and sister. Lee, although you are gone, I still feel your love and marvel in your ability to have been such a loving mother.

My many relatives with whom I grew up and who created a wonderful family support network for me. Special thanks to Scot for instilling a love of the Caps in my daughter throughout all the many games.

Jack, Judy, and Donna Martins, who have always been a second family to me. When we moved back to Virginia, you really took care of us. Jack and Judy, you are amazing parents and grandparents who have been such wonderful role models for me.

The Randall, Hampton, Zettelmoyer, Estrada, Clower and Donalty families, who I grew up with and spent a lot of time with in their homes. You helped raise me and nurtured me as one of your own. Special thanks to my dear friends, Aileen, Karyn, Beth, and Nancy, whose friendships I have cherished for a lifetime. Growing up with you made life easier.

My extended California families, the Kell, Chitiea, Tucker, Rosenbrach, Mullen, Katnick, Buccola, Welch and Shaw families, who were a constant support system. Special thanks to Rosemary for being like a sister. It has been so fun to raise our children together. I feel like Caitlin and Casey are my own.

My high school and college friends, who were my support network outside of my family. I was so fortunate to have you in my life. Special thanks to my DZ sisters, Val, Kirsten, Netty, and Lisa. You have been a great source of support and laughter in my life.

My playgroup moms, who helped raise my children and keep me sane. I appreciate you ladies.

The Fleagle and Kirby families who we have shared so many great memories and who have become our family in Virginia. Barbara, Stuart, Lori and Tom, it is has been so fun raising our children together and seeing them become so close. Also thank you, and Kathi and Dave Shultz, and Genie and John Coleman for helping David and me to have fun as a couple and nourish our relationship.

My neighbors and friends in Ashburn, who also raised my children and spent many hours in the cul-de-sac watching them play and grow up. Your advice and encouragement helped me immensely. Special thanks to the Kirby, Fleagle, Shultz, Flesch, Rolin, Brookbank, Schulein, Tripp, Penny, Herndon, Nowakowski, Morrison, Edeline, Apistolas, Weiss, Crammer, Pruitt, Kenney, Skelly, Long, and Gilmore families.

The teachers and staff at Stone Bridge High School, who not only supported me but also taught and cared for my children as they came through the school. It is a wonderful school filled with caring and loving people, and I am so glad my children experienced that. Special thanks to my social studies sisters, Amy Bria, Melissa Pruitt, Kelly Rosati, and Joany Windows. Also, to Tim Lucas for always being my sounding board, Andi Halpin for her sound advice and Pat Land and Darlene Brownlee for being my mentors.

My students at Stone Bridge High School, who taught me how to be a better parent. I learned a lot from you. Special thanks to my PEER kids; I truly love hanging with and learning so much from all of you. You are the most amazing young people.

The many attorneys I worked with at the Los Angeles Public Defender's Office and Dependency Court Legal Service. Your dedication to people, particularly children, is admirable, and I learned so much from you. Special thanks to Judge Michael Nash, who always looked after the children in his courtroom and demanded that all of us be our best for them.

The summer friends and families at Bethany Beach. You made my children feel like they were part of the community each summer. What a beautiful place for my children to spend each summer with great memories. Special thanks to the owners and staff at Mangos and Dickeys, who gave my children a place to work and allowed my children to be independent in a nurturing way.

The many teachers in my life, even some I have never met but learned so much from: Oprah Winfrey, Louise Hay, Wayne Dyer, Ester and Jerry Hicks (Abraham), and Dr. Oz.

The spiritual guidance that helped me write this book and put aside my fears.

All the wonderful parents out there who have touched my life and helped me be a better parent.

Contents

Acknowledgments v
Introduction xiii
Chapter 1 – My Journey 1
Chapter 2 – Routine, Structure, and Consistency 7
    Setting Up Daily Habits and Routines 14
Chapter 3 – Communication and Expectations 21
    Communication through the Ages 24
    Having the Tough Talks through the Teen Years 27
    Setting Reasonable Expectations and Sticking to Them 34
    Keeping Communication Healthy 37
    Learning How to Listen 39
Chapter 4 – Discipline and Consequences 43
    Why Do Children Need Discipline? 44
    Methods of Discipline 45
    Keeping Communication Healthy as We Discipline 48
    The Controversy Surrounding Corporal Punishment 50
    Final Thoughts about Discipline 55

Chapter 5 – Education 57
  Getting Involved 58
  Teaching Communication and Reading Skills 63
  Instilling a Love of Learning 65
  Setting Up Household Routines 67
  Setting Reasonable Goals 70
  Motivating Your Children to Succeed in School 71
Chapter 6 – Family Time, Dinner, and the Extended Family 75
  Making Family Time Sacred 76
  Dinnertime 78
  Creating and Keeping Family Traditions 81
  The Value of Time with Extended Family 82
  Leave a Lasting Memory 84
Chapter 7 – Having Choices and Figuring Out Problems 85
  Allowing and Teaching Choice as Children Grow and Mature 87
  "Being the Parent" and Limiting or Eliminating Choice 91
  Allowing Yourself to Gain Perspective and Lose Some Control 92
  Coaching Your Children through Adversity 95
  Stay Calm and Keep It in Perspective 96
Chapter 8 – Mistakes and Forgiveness 99
  Teaching Children How to Deal with Adversity 101
  Learning from the Veteran Pros 104
  Closing Thoughts 108
Chapter 9 – Role Model 111
  Modeling a Positive Attitude and Healthy Habits 112
  Sending the Right Messages about Substance Use and Abuse 115
  Modeling Emotional Strength and Anger Control 116
  Breaking the Cycle of Anger and Ending Bullying 119

Chapter 10 – Good Character, Respect, and Building Self-Esteem . 123
    Teaching, Instilling, and Modeling Good Character 124
    Building Self-Esteem 130
    Creating a Respectful, Empathetic Child 131

Chapter 11 – Children Are Different 135
    How to Nurture Your Child as an Individual 136
    Parenting Challenging Children 138
    Balancing the Needs of All Children 140
    Supporting Your Gay and Lesbian Children 142
    Keeping It Positive 144

Chapter 12 – Be Involved and Know Their Friends 147
    Supporting Your Children's Friendships 148
    How to Get Involved in Their Lives and
    Encourage Healthy Development 151
    Encouraging Kids' Sports Involvement 153
    How Healthy Involvement Can Ease Kids' Growing Pains
    (Or How Unhealthy Involvement Can Hinder It!) 154

Chapter 13 – Parents on the Same Page and Divorce 159
    Nurturing Sibling Relationships and Keeping Them Respectful ... 160
    Modeling Respect by Respecting Your Spouse 161
    Parenting as Partners 162
    Staying on the Same Page after a Divorce 166
    Avoiding Isolation and Reaching Out for Support 171

Chapter 14 – Love and Enjoy Your Children 173
    Communicating Your Love through Your Words and Messages 175
    Showing Your Love through Your Actions 176
    Getting Help so You Can Love Your Children Fully 178

Conclusion 181
Bibliography 183
Endnotes 187

Introduction

How can we be better parents? Why do some children turn out so successful and others struggle? These were two of the questions that drove me to interview parents of successful children. This book is a culmination of parenting wisdom, stories, and advice from the parents I interviewed, my observations as an attorney in the child abuse court and a teacher in high school, and even a record of some of my students' views on parenting.

The chapters are put in the order of importance that was reiterated over and over again by the parents I interviewed. From the first chapter until the end, the sequence was designed around the insistence of importance of the parents. All the information was seen as critical to a child's development, but some topics held more significance and were ordered accordingly, starting with the most important.

Whether you are a parent of a young child or a teenager or even a grandparent to one child or many, I believe the advice in this book can help your relationships become more positive and meaningful. Being the best parent you can be for your children is a gift you give them and yourself. Investing in them throughout their lives pays off when they become adults and are able to go out into the world and be independent, good, law-abiding citizens whom you can be proud of and enjoy being around.

It is time for all of us as parents to stop blaming the school systems and the government for our children's struggles and become better parents so our children can be successful. I am not saying as an active parent you cannot demand more from those institutions, but you can't rely on them to raise your children. You must be the best you can be so your children can be the best they can be.

In this book, I will use examples and personal stories. When referring to some former clients, students, and parents of children I represented, I changed certain identifying facts to protect their identities. If there appears to be a resemblance, it is coincidental. I wanted to do my best to protect the privacy and confidentiality of the people with whom I have worked and as well as the parents who shared their stories. Some stories were not changed if they were common knowledge in the community at large.

My hope is that by reading this book and implementing some of the advice herein, you will feel much more confident in your parenting and know that you are not alone. It is not a cliché that parenting is the toughest job you will ever have; educating yourself on how to do better is the first step to succeeding.

Chapter 1 - My Journey

"When you know better, you do better."[i] *(Maya Angelou)*

I never intended to write a book. That was not my mission when I set out to interview parents as I strove to understand the secret behind why some children become successful and others struggle. I was just curious to see if there were similarities between the parents of successful children. I have been fortunate throughout my years of teaching to work with some amazing young people. There have been several throughout my career who really made me say, "Wow, what did his or her parents do to raise such an exceptional individual?" Let me give you an example of what I am talking about. I remember an incident with a young man named Pat who really got me wondering.

He came into my classroom after school when the halls were quiet after the mad rush of the day. He walked in hesitantly wearing his baseball uniform and baseball cap slightly tilted off to the side of his head and looking a little like he needed something but wasn't quite sure he should walk through the door. In a very respectful tone and soft voice he said, "Mrs. Alison, can I speak to you about something?"

We sat in my classroom in the hard school chairs, facing each other as the warm afternoon light poured through the window. He proceeded to tell me about the difficulties he was having as the captain of the school baseball team because of struggles occurring between the players and the coach. I don't remember all the details he shared with me, but I do remember how torn he felt, like a piece of taffy being pulled between his loyalty to his teammates and his respect for the coach. He felt his duties to his team as the baseball captain were momentous, like a ship captain's duties to his crew on the high seas, and he wanted to build a bridge between the team and the coach so they could have a winning season.

We talked at length about the many ways he could help bring the team together. He even practiced some of his thoughts on me as if he were delivering the greatest speeches of his life, speeches like legendary baseball players Yogi Berra and Hank Aaron might have made to rouse their own teammates.

What amazed me so much, when I later reflected on this day, was that he never blamed anyone for what was occurring but instead felt the massive weight of responsibility to fix it. I was so impressed with his sincerity that day, with his determination and loyalty to both his team and coach, that I started asking myself questions. Where had he learned to think so responsibly and be so thoughtful of others while never really letting his own interests or ego get in the way? What did his parents do to help him turn out this way—to instill this genuine empathy for others and determination to be honorable whether he was in the classroom, on the baseball field, or even volunteering to mentor a young child? Where did this beautiful, sincere smile, sparkling eyes, and infectious laughter come from? See, he didn't just have good character; he exuded it from every pore. What had his parents done to raise him to be this way? He was not the only one; there have been many other students over the years, and I had to know what made these young people turn out this way.

Inspired, I set out to interview the parents of exceptional children, with Pat's mother being one of the first. What I found was remarkable. As we spoke, I discovered there really *were* things these parents had done in common to produce these very uncommon results. As we spoke, they relayed over and over again the same key principles—the importance of routine, structure, and consistency; communication and expectations; discipline and consequences; education; family time; having choices and figuring out problems; mistakes and forgiveness; being a role model; instilling good character; knowing children are different; being involved in their lives; having both parents be on the same page; and loving your children. I was astounded. With a treasure of parental advice, I felt more compelled than ever that it was my duty—the culmination of a lifetime mission to help children and families—to write this book and share their secrets.

"An author?" one might ask. I even asked it of myself. See, I am on my third profession, of sorts—first lawyer, then teacher, now author. But there is one thing I have always known, one thing that has spurred all of my career choices: I feel a deep, protective connection to children. It's like if I were a "superhero," I would have a *C* on my cape for children. I can't explain this deep need to help and protect kids, but it is who I am; it's something in my DNA that drives me.

It first reared its head when I started babysitting at eleven years old and continued into my high school years when I got a job at a preschool assistant. It surfaced in eighth grade as sharp, physical pain in my heart when shown pictures of abused children in civics class—bruised and battered bodies, cigarette-burned skin, and malnourished beings. The familiar gnawing crept in again and continued on as I represented children ranging from drug babies to abused and abandoned teenagers as an attorney. See, as an attorney, I thought I could continue my mission—my superhero crusade—especially after I landed my dream job as an attorney representing children in the child abuse court in LA.

However, with my own growing family, a demanding job requiring a long commute, and a sobering, I-get-the meaning-of-life-now wake-up call in the form of a 6.9 earthquake in California in 1994, something had to change. I knew this superhero needed to tighten her other cape, the one with an *M* for Mom, and I moved my family back to Virginia to focus on my own children. I joined the powerful army of stay-at-home moms, determined to fight for my own children, until I realized there was another way I could serve children while still meeting the needs of my own kids: I would teach. With my home within walking distance of the school and my kids attending the school where I taught, I knew I had finally found a way to merge my causes—two capes nicely melding into one.

See, I've always known that through it all, whether representing clients, teaching social studies, or fighting for the needs of an abused child, I am drawn to these young people like bees to honey. This book, one that culminated from extensive interviews with wildly successful parents and teens, finally allows me a forum to fight for families on a larger scale. It allows me to help you—parents who want their children to be responsible, happy, self-actualized, independent, law-abiding citizens—to learn from the successes and failures of those I interviewed.

When I started, I did not know what would come out of these interviews. In the beginning, I just knew I had to talk to these parents, starting with my well-intentioned baseball player Pat's mom. I had anticipated talking for about an hour, but I did not know how powerful these interviews would be, with each usually lasting about two hours as we sipped lattés or tea at Starbucks or conspired in my deserted, after-school classroom. They all had so much to say, opening up to me and sharing their secrets; I knew from the first interview I was hooked.

One of the first questions I asked each parent was "What is the one thing you would tell a new parent is the most important thing in raising a child?' I also asked "How do you help your child be successful in school?" and "How do you instill good character?" I also tried to go deeper and ask why they felt the way they did, often laughing and crying with them as they told me their stories because the emotions were so palpable.

As I processed all the life lessons I had learned through my interviews, I realized I would have loved to have known all this when I was raising my children. The old "superhero gene" swooped in again. I might be able to save the day for another parent, I realized, and in doing so, I could further realize my mission to help children by reaching out to so many parents.

Some of you may be parents from dysfunctional families who have picked up this book in the hopes of doing better. I hope with all my heart this helps. I have seen firsthand as an attorney and as a teacher how difficult it is to break the cycle, but it can be done. Through the wisdom of these parents, I hope you find something of value in this book. Maybe you are a parent already doing a good job and just want to know more. I hope this information resonates with you, and you find some things to help you do even better. I applaud you all for trying to do better.

In this country, there are just way too many children struggling, and as parents, we can help by doing a little better ourselves. We can't just expect the schools to help our children be successful; instead, it is our duty as parents to be the best we can be to help our children be the best they can be. As Maya Angelou said, "When you know better, you do better."

This book is a culmination of my life observations and experiences, the wisdom of the parents I interviewed and ones I have observed throughout my life, and some insight from my students and young clients. I am excited for you to continue reading.

Chapter 2 - Routine, Structure, and Consistency

"Children Learn What They Live."[ii] (Dorothy Law Neite)

We broke her! We broke our one-month-old daughter! That is what I thought the day she would not stop crying. Jocelyn was just four weeks old, and the entire family was going to Disney Land for my mother's birthday. My older brother and sister each had one-year-old boys, and they were eager to take them to Disney Land. My mother always talked about how hard it was to go Disney Land the first time, because she was by herself and she wanted to go with her entire family for her birthday. How could I say no? My daughter Jocelyn was a good baby, and I thought she would just eat and sleep through the park. How hard could it be?

She was perfect all day, like a little doll. Everyone remarked about what a good baby she was. But when we all said good-bye at the end of the day and got in our cars, something went terribly wrong. In the quiet of the car, Jocelyn started crying and would not stop. No amount of consoling, rocking, feeding, or changing would stop the crying. We had broken her. We were new parents and so distraught that we pulled into the nearest emergency care center to have her seen.

When we checked in with the nurse, who asked what was wrong with our baby, we explained that she wouldn't stop crying. At this point, I also was crying. What had I done to our perfect baby? By the time we saw the doctor, both Jocelyn and I were exhausted from crying, and my poor husband was beside himself not knowing what to do for the two girls in his life. The doctor calmly came over and picked up Jocelyn, and in his caring hands, she instantly stopped crying. He looked her over gently and said, "She is fine." He went on to look at me and say, "I think Mom is the one who may need some help," in a very kind manner.

He proceeded to tell me that she was just over stimulated from the day and that her routine had been taken away, so she felt a little off. He explained the importance of routine to a baby and let me know that she would be just fine tomorrow when she returned to her normal day with its consistent routines. I was so relieved and realized how important her daily schedule and routine was to her.

One of the crucial things you can do for your children when they are born and throughout their lives is to set up and maintain consistent routines and structures. In fact, one of the most important points the parents I interviewed kept reinforcing was the importance of structure. According to these parent experts, parenting is a lifelong adventure that starts when children are born, an adventure that's both exhausting and rewarding. As they made clear, good parents never get a day off. They often feel like they are doing it all wrong, but they just have to keep at it.

As parents, they maintain, we want our children to come out of our parenting and be, to state it simply, people we would like to know and be around. It starts from day one; parents must be present in their children's lives and give up their selfish ways. One can't be too tired to parent. When children are young, it can be very tiring because they need so much, but that changes as they become more independent. It is the groundwork you do when they are young that will help you when they reach the difficult teenage years.

Although children may balk at the idea of structure, consistent routines give them a feeling of security so they can grow to their full potential. Structure makes a child feel comforted because he knows what to expect, the parents explained. Every one of us needs the basic structure of eight hours sleep, eight hours of school or work, and eight hours of free time. If we learn to set up our children's lives in such a way, they know what to expect each day.

One parent relayed a story about her nephew who had very little routine or structure in his life. When he was about three, he was not made to sit at the table when he ate dinner; instead, he just ate all over the house like a stray cat. At night, he was allowed to run around the house still in the clothes he wore all day until he dropped and fell asleep from exhaustion. One night he literally slept under the dining room table, his little body curled up on the floor. The next morning it was discovered he had peed on the carpet where he slept, and his mother yelled at him as if he should have known better. But he didn't know any better. He was not taught important routines, like to go to the bathroom before going to sleep. As a result, he was just a mess.

Working in the child abuse court when my children were very young gave me some insight about being a good parent. I witnessed some inappropriate parenting, but I also had cases that really took me awhile to figure out what had gone wrong. One of the cases that truly baffled me was also one that made me realize how important routine and structure were. I represented a young boy of about fourteen years old who would not go to school. I picked up the case after he had been out of his home for several months and in a group home. He seemed like a nice young man; however, he was clearly not motivated when it came to school.

The group home he was in had structure and routines, so he did attend school in their care. The judge was willing to send him back home if he and his mom promised that he would attend school every day. They both assured me he would go each day, and I relayed that to the judge. I remember distinctly the judge warning him that if he became truant again, he would end up back in the group home.

As you can guess, the minute he went home he slipped back into his old habits and stopped going to school. As the reports came into court from the social worker that this was happening, the judge grew angry and threatened to send him back to the group home. I, being a young, naive parent with a two-year-old and another baby on the way, volunteered to go one morning to the house and get him off to school. I mean, how hard could it be? Just wake him up and get him to school, right?

I will never forget going to the house that morning; I can still remember it vividly even twenty years later. I arrived at the house and Mom let me in, all chipper and awake, saying something like, "Good luck trying to get him up. I have tried everything." She did not seem mad or angry, just matter-of-fact, like she had given up. I headed down the hall to the room the boy shared with his older brother. As I went into the room, a little two-year-old boy, who I later found out was their younger brother, was running around screaming "f——k you" like it was the most natural thing in the world. Mom just looked at me, laughed, and said, "Oh, the boys taught him that. They think it is funny to hear him swear." She just shook her head like she felt there was nothing she could do about it and left me to go into the room alone.

As an attorney representing children, I tried really hard not to pass judgment on people, especially since I was a new parent myself, but this situation just seemed so bizarre to me. Needless to say, my attempts to get this young man up and to school were futile. I tried everything, even reminding him he would go back to the group home, but nothing worked. I was there for about an hour, trying everything I knew to do at the time, and nothing worked. Even my attempt at inspirational talks did not work; he was determined to win at all costs. I was shocked that I left that morning without getting him off to school. I had thought I was going to be able to just go in that house and show that mom how it was done. Instead, as I was leaving, she just smiled at me and said something to the effect of this is just how it is and nothing can change it.

Now I know what a lot of you may be thinking. I know my own father would be saying something like, "I would give him a reason to go to school" and back it up with a stern voice. Most of you may even be shocked that this case was in the child abuse court. You probably think most of the cases I dealt with were actually physical abuse, but they weren't. I saw so many different forms of abuse. In this case, the law requires parents to send their children to school. As a teacher in Virginia today, I know that if parents do not send their children to school, they could end up in court themselves and charged with a crime. But at this time in California, it was the child who was taken out of the home because Mom could not get him to school. I went back to court and had to report that I too had failed to get my client to school, and he was sent back to the group home. In this instance, the judge had to do the parenting in this young man's life when the mother fell short of her duties.

This case really bothered me. I could not figure out what went wrong until I thought about the two-year-old boy running around the house cussing. While I was shocked by this behavior, Mom thought it was kind of funny. She seemed to think it was harmless and did not do anything about it. But it was that two-year-old and my client who taught me the importance of structure, routine, and starting young. I learned that it is important to teach the behaviors you want to see when they are teenagers and adults when they are at the young ages of two and three years old, because what may look cute and harmless at two years old won't look that way when they are teenagers. Instead, the routines and structures you set can help them be successful in life later.

According to the parents I interviewed, being consistent may even teach children time management techniques that they will use the rest of their lives. When these routines are not in place at an early age, parents are in trouble when kids are twelve and thirteen and testing their independence. Children need to have some basic things they do, routines as natural as breathing that they don't question. If these structures are not in place at a young age, it is very difficult to start introducing them when they are older.

The teenage years are tough, and children are confused about what is happening to them. If parents have structures in place and life has some consistency, it will be easier on both the children and the parents. Structure also helps to show children boundaries and teaches them to take care of themselves. Some of the parents I spoke to felt they did not have routines and structure when they grew up, and they wanted to make sure their own children had more consistency in their lives. It also relays the message that their parents care. Parents can say "I love you", but it is their daily actions that have the most impact, as was reiterated by successful parents time and time again throughout my interviews.

Having said all this, there is a caveat. With everything a parent does, you must do it with *balance*. There is a fine line in everything you do, like balancing on a tightrope. Too much structure and routine can be a negative factor, caging in your child. Children need freedom to develop into their own authentic people; too much structure and routine can take away from that creative self-development that all children crave. Parents have to set up the basics for children to learn, but they can't make it so routine and structured that children can't learn to be independent. Instead, as was made clear to me through countless interviews, the parents' job is to create independent, good citizens. Children have to learn and make mistakes in order to understand how to cope with all of life's situations. Some children need more structure than others, and some routines that work for one child do not work for another. Parents, then, need to be flexible and willing to adjust.

Furthermore, another important point reinforced by successful parents is to not schedule out the kids' entire lives. They need play time or free time just to do what they want. We are in a society today where children rarely just get to be free to do whatever they choose. They have soccer practice, violin lessons, Mandarin Chinese lessons, and dance. You may think this is a joke, but this is the life of some children, and it becomes too overwhelming. Being involved in some extracurricular activity is good for children to learn to be on a team and make friends, but over scheduling a child is just too stressful. They burn out by the time they start middle and high school. Instead, let them play! I will be the first to admit if there was a special occasion or opportunity for my children, I would not cut it short because they had to be in bed by eight o'clock. I was not so rigid; instead, I was flexible and adjusted in the moment. On the other hand, I have seen young parents go overboard with routines. Although I think structure and routine are important for children, I also agree with the parents interviewed that there has to be balance.

As a teacher, I saw a situation where parents seemed too structured and controlling. One of my students was so controlled by her parents she began suffering from depression and cutting herself on purpose. She would actually cut at her wrists because she had no control in her life. Her parents would not let her out of their sight. She was a senior in high school, and her parents would not let her go anywhere without them because they worried about her being alone. They were very protective and had her life structured out so they were with her all the time. For example, when she wanted to go to the movies with her friends, they would go to the movie also and be in the back. Although these parents were well intentioned, parents need to teach children to be independent so they can function on their own. It is not healthy for a child to be too dependent on their parents. The lesson is *balance*. Have structure and routine but not so much that it does not let your child grow into an independent, functioning adult. The routines should actually be designed to help them be independent, not dependent.

Even according to the teens I interviewed, structure and routine provide them with security. They urged parents to be flexible, though, so they could learn that change is fine also. We need to feel safe in change too, they maintained. They also asked parents not to have so much structure that it caused their children to become too dependent, because children need to learn to be independent as well.

Setting Up Daily Habits and Routines

Morning Routine

Setting up a morning routine that is both calm and gets children excited for school will help them be more successful in school. For example, start by waking children up for a good, nutritious breakfast. Also, make sure to give them enough time to get ready for school without feeling rushed and stressed, because it can make all the difference in whether they have a good day at school or not.

Teaching children that they need to get to school on time at a young age will help when they are teenagers; as a result, you won't have to deal with tardiness and phone calls home because they are always late. Remember that it starts when they are young, not when they start high school. It's also important to remember that if you are a parent of a teenager who is struggling, it is never too late to start.

One of the parents I spoke to, a guidance counselor, remembered a meeting with a fifteen-year-old student and his parents, and the problem basically came down to the fact that the child was acting out because he'd had no structure in his life and could not function in school. The parents wanted to know what they could do at this point to help him be successful. The counselor wanted to tell them that it was a little too late to be setting this up when he was fifteen, but she held herself back. In short, a fifteen-year-old already has established patterns and routines, and it is more difficult to change those patterns when she is older.

Daytime Routines

The importance of routine also applies to the time after school. Setting up a routine of getting homework done before children go out and play sets the tone that school is important. It is okay if they come home, have a snack, and relax for a short time, but by telling your children they must do their homework before they go out and play, you send the message that school is a top priority. If they get used to doing this every day in elementary school, they will be used to doing it by middle and high school; you won't even have to stand over them to ensure it is done. It becomes second nature, because it is the routine they are used to, like brushing their teeth every evening.

Conversely, imagine coming home from a long day at school not knowing what to expect. Every day you get a different parent (personality) greeting you at the door to a different situation. This would be very stressful for anyone, especially for a young child. Let's face it: knowing what to expect in your environment is comforting, and predictable routines provide this security for children.

Although many parents wonder whether they are harming their children through enrolling them in day care, one of my students learned many of her routines from her daycare experience growing up. She understood that some parents needed to have their children in day care when they were young. For her, it was a positive experience where she not only had routines and structures but also learned how to make friends. She felt it helped her be more independent as a teenager. When she was home with her parents, they were very present in her life, so she did not feel like she missed out on anything.

In addition to homework, another important daytime routine is dinnertime. In fact, every parent I interviewed felt this was an important routine to set up in the day, because it is often the one time families get to connect and spend time together during the busy day. This important daytime routine will be handled in a separate chapter later in the book.

Bedtime Routines

Everyone has heard of the three *B*s: bath, book, and bed. Or, when you have an infant, it is more like bath, book, bottle, and bed. This is the evening routine for most children to help them get ready for bed. When they are old enough, it expands into something like bath, brush teeth, book, prayers, and bed. Whatever your routine, find one that works for you so your children have a nightly routine that helps them go to sleep, because getting a good night's sleep is essential for all people, young and old, to allow the body to regenerate. Setting up effective bedtime routines starts when children are born, really, and if you start young, it becomes part of the fabric of who they are. They don't even realize that they learned a routine; it is just woven into who they have become.

In fact, one of the biggest challenges of new parents is teaching their children to fall asleep at night. The dreaded nightly game parents play with children to get them to sleep is one that resonates with many parents. The scenario is usually something like this: The parent is tired and exhausted from a long day at work but also feels guilty about being away from the child all day. When the child begs "one more book" or "sleep with me," how can the parent resist? And so begins the nightly game that can become a literal nightmare for all involved—a nightmare that shines a spotlight on the need to establish and maintain successful bedtime routines.

Even with the bath, book, bottle, and bed routine, children have to learn to put themselves to sleep. This does not apply to new infants who need to be fed, changed, and picked up when they cry, of course, but when children are about four to six months old, they really need to start learning to put themselves to sleep. Many of us rocked our babies, played music, drove them around in the car, and told them stories just to get them to sleep, but at some point in their young lives, they will have to learn how to drift off to sleep on their own.

All children are different, and some will be easier than others when it comes to teaching them to fall asleep. All three of my children were different, and it was exhausting trying to figure out what worked with each of them. With both my daughters, I finally had to do what I fondly call the three-night rule. This is a technique the experts suggest, and it really does work. For at least three nights, you are not allowed to take the child out of the crib even when he cries for you. You can go into the room and tell him he is fine, but you can't pick him up. This will be a very long ordeal at first, because the child is looking to his parents to help him fall asleep, and instead the parent is trying to teach him to do it on his own.

When I used this method with my daughters, I remember the crying getting pretty intense and lasting a long time. Eventually, they did fall asleep, and I did it again the next night. By the third night, it really did work. Just remember: when following this method, if you pick the child up, it is all over, and you have to start from night one again. Don't give in. Just keep going in the room and reassuring him that he is fine. This is some tough parenting, but if the child can learn to put himself to sleep, it will be a big payoff for you and him later in life. There are many techniques, advice books, and websites to help you do this. Just know almost every parent goes through this, and it is hard. You will get through this.

Routine and structure were part of my life as a child, so when I became a parent, it was second nature for me to try to provide that structure for my own children, especially at bedtime. I imagine that is the case for many other parents as well. I worried when my children were little that maybe I took my routines too seriously. One example of this was when my children were in elementary school. I was very structured when it came to making sure they went to bed at a decent time so they would be up and ready for school each morning. After dinner, we did the routine of bath, book, and bed. I did not let them watch TV before bed on school nights. They were to be in bed around eight o'clock, and after we read together, they could continue reading in bed if they were not tired yet, but lights had to be out by nine. They usually were asleep right away, because they were exhausted from the day, but it was tougher in the spring. As the daylight hours grew longer, it was harder to get them to want to go to sleep around eight o'clock, but I still felt they needed enough sleep for school. I would tell them they could be in their rooms reading, but the issue became tough when some of the other neighbor children were still outside playing. My children could hear them through the screened windows playing until nine o'clock, nine thirty, and sometimes even ten o'clock at night. I even heard the comments from well-meaning friends and neighbors that "the Alison children were in bed by eight o'clock on school nights." At the time, I really questioned myself. Was I being too rigid? Should I just let them go out and play like the others? I didn't give in, and to my children's credit, they really didn't complain much.

In the end, I never had an issue with my children being able to get to school on time, even in high school. As a teacher, I see this become a major issue for some children in the high school years. I see students with high GPAs coming to school late and ending up in ISR (in-school restriction) because of countless tardies. Here are intelligent students who can't get to school by nine o'clock in the morning. I wonder what happens to them when they graduate and get a job; I worry that without routines in place, their chances for future success are affected. It is the little routines you set up when they are young that set them up for life.

Children's lives can be chaotic, especially when they start school. At school, they must be on their best behavior, and it can be very exhausting for them to be constantly going all day. However, home should be a place where they don't have to constantly watch themselves; it needs to be a safe place for them to be themselves, where they can feel secure and know what to expect. If they come home to no routines and chaos, they never get a break from the busy day, and in turn, life is constantly changing and causing them stress.

I know establishing routines and structures when children are young can be time consuming and exhausting, but it will pay off. In fact, even a fifty-year study on families taken on by Syracuse University found that "Family routines and rituals were found to be related to parenting competence, child adjustment, and marital satisfaction." [iii] So, make your home a safe, nurturing place where your children know what to expect each day. Every now and then throw in some surprises so you don't become too rigid. Have breakfast for dinner or stay up late on the weekends, but put the routines and structures in place for your child's day-to-day life.

Chapter 3 - Communication and Expectations

"Deep listening is miraculous for both listener and speaker. When someone receives us with open-hearted, non-judging, intensely interested listening, our spirits expand."[iv] *(Sue Patton Thoele)*

There is a letter inside nearly every teenager I meet. It goes a little something like this.

Dear Mom and Dad,

I know you might not always think it's true, but I do love you and I want a good relationship with you, although I may not always show that.

Sometimes I feel like you don't appreciate me. I am a good kid, but you get all upset because I don't clean my room. I don't do drugs, and I work hard in school. I am a good person—isn't that enough? Sometimes it feels like nothing is good enough, like even I am not good enough. I need to hear you tell me that I am good enough, even if I am not perfect in your eyes.

Please talk to me, but don't nag me. Constant nagging feels like a put down; it makes me feel like I am not good enough. For example, by high school, I know to do my homework, so you don't have to keep reminding me.

I know you get angry with me, but if you always scream at me, I become numb to it and it doesn't have any effect. If you are always disappointed in me, I stop caring how you feel, so please only tell me you are disappointed in serious circumstances. It hurts to hear you say that, even when I may deserve to hear it.

Don't overreact and get all upset if I tell you things about my friends that you may not approve of, and please don't hold the things I tell you against my friends or me later on. In the end, it may be better that I don't know everything you did when you were young. Understand that you don't need to know everything about my life either.

Instead, listen and be there for me. When I come to you to talk, just let me vent. I am not always looking for advice; instead, sometimes I just need a place to talk freely. People need at least one person in their lives who will listen to them. If I can't talk to you, I will try to find someone else who will listen, like my friends, my friend's parents, a teacher, or a coach, but I really want that person to be you.

You need to parent me and tell me when I am messing up, even though I may not like it at the time. I need a parent, not a friend. I need you to keep me in check and let me know if you think I am making the wrong decisions, but even when I do make the wrong decisions, please always be there for me.

Please do set expectations; don't just let me do whatever I want. When you have expectations for me, it makes me feel like you care. Help me set goals and help me find ways to reach them. Please do have high expectations for me, but don't have ridiculous ones that are not realistic.

Mom and Dad, I may not appreciate all you do, but later on I will. I know that some decisions are ones you must make, but at least let me feel like my views matter sometimes. In the meantime, talk to me and educate me about the world. Be open and share things with me as I try to grow up. Let's just keep on talking.

Love,

Your Child

As mothers and fathers explained to me over coffee and water bottle chats, teaching your children to communicate and really listening to them when they talk are two of the greatest gifts you can give them. Communication is the way to show you value your children, because when you really listen to your children, it validates who they are. This point, one stressed by successful parents, was one of the most important to emerge during my long stretch of interviews.

Allison Merkle Alison

Communication through the Ages

Communication starts at a young age. Talk to your babies—point to things and tell them the words. Their little brains are forming so fast, and they can learn from you if you take the time and care to teach them. One of my favorite memories as a young parent was watching my father carrying around his grandchildren for hours as he pointed to different objects and told them their names. Both he and whatever child he was holding at the time seemed so at peace and so connected, like they were communicating without a discussion. Reading to your child from birth is another way to develop those communication skills.

The "terrible twos" are a real phenomenon, although this behavior can come as early as eighteen months or as late as three years old. Some children have a more difficult time than others, and these troubles can arise at different ages in different children. The common tantrums can be about the frustration that comes when they are unable to communicate their needs, or it can be about their need to learn to calm themselves down when they are upset about not getting their own way. Either way, learning how to communicate at an early age can help alleviate this behavior. Tell them to use their words when they are frustrated and feeling like having a tantrum. Just know this period will pass. However, it is important to get it under control and not ignore it, because it will creep back up in the middle school years when they are struggling again to figure it all out.

As parents explained to me countless times, parents need to help their children express themselves when they are young so they can communicate. Gone are the days of the statement, "Children are meant to be seen but not heard." Instead, teach your children that they have voices that deserve to be heard. Teaching them the "I" message about how they feel can help them express themselves. For example, teach them to say, "I feel …" instead of "You made me feel …" The first way validates how they feel and cannot be discounted, while the later is accusatory and can cause others to become defensive.

It is very difficult to grow up in a family where all you hear is not to do this or that "because I said so." When children constantly hear this, it shuts down communication. Instead, explain to your children why and let them know you are just not saying no because you want to control them. Let them know it is okay for them to disagree with you and others but that they must do so in a respectful way.

Talking to them at a young age can help educate them on important life matters and teach them communication skills. For example one of the parents I spoke to offered that if you see them swinging and they jump off in a dangerous way, you can say something like this, "Wow, that looked like fun, but don't do it again because that is dangerous. I would be sad if you got hurt. If you want to do flips like that, we can look into taking a gymnastics class so you can do that safely." Other times, like when you are watching TV, enjoying a movie, or reading a book together, talk about the moral of the story and discuss the issues addressed. This can be really important when dealing with issues of drinking, smoking, drugs, and sex as they get older. Have those tough conversations.

When your children start school, do more than just ask them how their days went when they come home. Nine times out of ten you will get the response "fine" unless you ask different types of specific questions. Instead, ask things like "Who did you sit with at lunch?" or "What did you do at recess?" These are both things they like about the day, and as a result, they may be more willing to talk about them. This may just get the conversation going and lead to a deeper conversation. Teaching your children to talk about their days will help them learn to communicate more effectively, and it will give you insight into their lives and their schooling.

When listening to your child, repeat what you hear her say to make sure you truly understand how she feels. This can be done by saying something like "It sounds like you are mad at your friend for not inviting you over." On the same note, always be sure to have her clarify what you say, because she may have interpreted it differently that you intended.

Also, as children mature, communicate with them about important life issues, like money and dealing with adversity. Teach them about the things you value. When they are young, you will not want to over burden them with the harsh realities of the world, but as they get older, let them learn from you. You teach through your words and actions.

One way you can introduce your children to important concerns is to have family talks on how to deal with important family matters. Let your children have a voice, even if the final decision on how to handle the issue rests with you and your spouse. By opening this line of communication, you are teaching them to handle life situations in a positive way. So when it comes to sibling squabbles, don't be quick to fix everything. Teach them to talk to each other instead, just like during a family meeting, and work it out between themselves. If you step in every time they have a fight, you will have to referee everything.

You can't control everything in your child's life, but you can be someone who is there to listen. Realize, though, that some children may feel more comfortable talking to one parent over the other. Don't take offense if you are not the one they are coming to; instead, be glad they have someone to talk to.

Having the Tough Talks through the Teen Years

In middle school, during those awkward teenage years, children are really struggling with hormonal changes, independence, and relationships. What I didn't know when my own children were teenagers but know now is that it is part of their life journey to pull away from you and start down their road to independence. It is a tough time, but if your child can communicate with you, it is easier.

I remember how it felt so vividly—the looks of embarrassment on my children's teenage faces at anything I did. Even the simple act of asking the checkout lady at the grocery store how she was doing brought on a quick "Oh, Mom, why do you ask so many questions?" I can still hear the sound my children made at this age when they did not like what I had to say to them. It sounded like a tire was leaking.

This was a particularly hard time for me with my oldest daughter, because I had never experienced this before. I didn't know there would come a time when she would return to me as a supportive, kind person—one not embarrassed by everything I did. Instead, at the time, I was a little heartbroken that she was pulling away and growing up. Couldn't I keep her a young child forever? We had, instead, arrived at a point where we just could not communicate with each other, as if we spoke totally different languages.

It was the homework a teacher gave my daughter in middle school that got us communicating again. The assignment was for both of us. We were to read a book together and write back and forth in a journal what we thought of each chapter. I forget the title of the book, but I remember it had a lot of life lessons in it that we could write about. We became so caught up in the book that communication just came naturally to us again. I can't help but think this very smart teacher knew exactly what she was doing assigning this particular homework to her middle school students. I tend to think she knew we all need a little help in these treacherous waters of teenage-hood, and she was throwing us a life preserver with that assignment.

What I learned through those experiences with my eldest daughter is that teenage years are very challenging, so if you have set up good communication earlier in their lives, it helps. Just know this teenage time will pass, and you can get through it. Never avoid the tough conversations; it is better to talk about them than hide them.

To illustrate, at some point, your school-age children will come to you and talk about their teachers, much like how we talk about our bosses from time to time. Somewhere along the way in school, they will have a teacher they do not like. When they feel like the teacher is mean or doing things wrong, just listen. They need to vent, just like we adults vent about the trying people and situations in our own lives. It does not mean you have to agree or fix things; instead, just listen. They must learn to respect authority, but it is okay to challenge it in a respectful way. Just remember not to let the communication always be about complaining and finding fault, because you don't want your children to grow up being negative. If you feel they are becoming this way, talk to them about it and help them be more positive.

It is important to really listen if your children say they are being bullied. Dealing with bullying and mean people is a part of life, and many children and even adults will experience this at some point in their lives. Validate their feelings by saying something like, "I am sorry you are going through this, and I know it is hard. You can get through this." They don't necessarily need you to fix things for them. They need you to really listen and show them that they are not alone. The best thing you can do is to help them figure out a way to handle the bullies they may encounter. For example, you can role-play with them on how they can handle bullies. You can also encourage them to have their friends around them to limit the bullying. Even brainstorm alternatives to help them come up with a plan.

At some point, if the bullying continues or it is dangerous, you may have to step in and contact someone. If the bullying is at school, you can contact a guidance counselor, teacher, or administrator without your child or the bully knowing. You can even let that person know that you would like to help your child resolve things on his or her own and that you are just letting him know about the situation. If you can help your children learn techniques to handle bullying on their own, it will not only make them feel powerful, but it will also help them grow. Don't be so quick to jump in and save them, and when they are in pain, sometimes you just need to sit with them. It is difficult to watch your children suffer, but being there for them and listening is the best thing you can do for them. They will feel powerful knowing they are loved and you are there for them.

The teenage years can also be difficult, because children are getting a lot of peer pressure to do inappropriate things they know they are not suppose to do. Make sure to sit them down and talk to them about making correct choices; have those tough talks. Don't just brush it under the rug. Know that they will make mistakes and help them learn from their mistakes by talking to them and letting them know that we all mess up but we can learn from it. Also, let them know they can use you as the excuse to get them out of difficult situations. You can even set up a code word that they can use to call you for a ride home if they are in a tough spot.

When it comes to taking about drinking, you need to tell your children it is illegal under the age of twenty-one. However, many of the parents I spoke to knew their children were doing it; we all know drinking is going on in college. Many of us could legally drink beer in college, and we did. Also, many of us feel it should be legal for eighteen, nineteen, and twenty year olds, so we add to the mixed message about drinking in college. Let your children know that drinking is not a prize of adulthood; be clear that drinking and driving will not be tolerated. You need to reiterate this message often and clearly. Make a pact with your child that if he finds himself in a situation where he has been drinking and needs a ride home, you will pick him up—no questions asked. There will be no repercussions, just call. Tell your children not get in the car drunk and drive and don't get in the car with someone else who has been drinking.

Be clear on your feelings about drugs and that they are not tolerated. Many children are in the D.A.R.E. program at school in fourth grade. This can open the conversation up for you to talk to them, but don't let the conversation stop there. When talking about drugs, give examples of people you know and how doing drugs messed up their lives. Keep talking about drug use and abuse all through their school years. Keep an extra vigilant watch during the middle and early high school years when experimentation with drugs often begins. You need to key into your children; you will get a sense that something is wrong if you continue communicating with them.

One parent relayed a story about his son being friends with a boy who started doing poorly in school in eighth grade. His grades dropped significantly, which was a big indicator that something was wrong. He was experimenting with drugs and not doing well, sending many signals, but the parents of this boy did not key in and instead let the signals pass unnoticed. In the end, the young man ended up being arrested.

Another parent listened as her child told her about a thirteen-year-old friend who was having sex with her boyfriend. She had developed early and was in a long-term relationship with the boy, but in the end, the friend was not ready for this relationship and was hurt when it ended. The parent just listened and did not pass judgment on the girl or give advice; instead, she just letting her child vent without having to be defensive.

Finally, if your child ever comes to you and tells you that someone has sexually abused her, even if she says it was a family member, you must give her the benefit of the doubt and listen. When I worked in the child abuse court, all the cases I saw involving sexual abuse were perpetrated by someone the child knew—fathers, stepfathers, brothers, uncles, and even one mother. Even through my criminal experience, the majority of cases involved someone the child had a relationship with. I tell you this because we are so busy teaching our children to watch out for strangers, we may be missing the real danger.

You don't want to scare your children and have them worrying about being molested, but you should teach your children that they should not keep secrets from you and that you will always be there for them no matter what. If you do have a child who comes to you and tells you this has happened, you have to believe her, even if it is unimaginable. If you question her motives, don't let on when she originally tells you. You must support her and get help to figure out the situation. It is not your job to play judge and jury but to support your child. If your child is accusing a father or stepfather, your loyalty must be with the child. You can let your spouse know you are confused, but you must support your child at the outset.

Telling someone about sexual abuse is not only difficult; it is truly a brave thing to do. Most children don't speak up and hope it just goes away. They are embarrassed and ashamed and blame themselves. I saw too many cases in the court system where the mother sided with her spouse instead of her child. The Department of Children's Services had no choice but to take the child from the mother, because with that view, she could not protect her child. If you are in a situation where you don't feel financially or emotionally secure to leave your spouse, get help from the local women's shelter in your area. They will help you and your child. You cannot ignore the signs or your child's words that this is going on. You must get her out of the situation and get help. No child deserves to be abused in any way, and it is your job to protect her. If you have an open line of communication, she will know she can come to you if she ever feels uncomfortable about something.

One other important point to consider is that you need to communicate how you feel if you are not comfortable with something your children are asking you to do. For example, if they ask to sleep at someone's house whose parents you do not know or to go to a party somewhere you're not familiar with, tell your children that until you get all the facts and feel comfortable with the situation, they can't go. Let them know you trust them, but that you do not want to put them in a situation that is dangerous or that they are not ready to handle.

To help you feel better about the situation, call the parents whose house they want to go to and speak to them. When you first tell your children you have to call the parents, they may put up a fuss and say they will be humiliated. However, parents actually appreciate calls from concerned parents. Once you make the call and feel comfortable with the situation, then let them go.

It is difficult to tell your child not to do something when one of the parents does it. For example, if one parent smokes, you may not want your children to smoke, but by watching a parent do it, the odds are greater they will grow up and do it. You are their role model. This does not mean you can't still talk to them about how you feel and let them know that you don't want them to do it. One mother wished she'd had the courage to talk about his issue with her son. She did not talk about it, and he grew and smoked, just like his father. Be honest and tell them how you feel about things.

Even when children don't want to talk and seem to be pushing you away, stay involved and keep communicating. At some point, they will talk to you again. Never give up. If your teenager is out of control, communicate that you need to work things out. You will need to find out what is important to him. Find the carrot, so to speak, that gives him incentive to do better. In the teenage years, the phone and the ability to drive are powerful carrots.

When your child does come talk to you about a problem, listen. When he is going through tough times, there is an opportunity for growth. Problems are really opportunities to grow. Have your child ask, "What am I suppose to learn from this?" The saying "when one door closes another one opens" is true. Having someone to talk to is important and really is what he needs. He really doesn't need you to fix things.

The car is a safe place to have these difficult conversations. You can say anything, and it does not leave the area. Time in the car is a forced intimate situation where children can't run away. Let them know that what they talk about won't be held against them. Don't always give advice. Just listen. One parent remembered being in the car with her teenage daughter when her daughter asked to go on birth control. After she made every attempt not to drive them off the road, she calmly talked to her about the consequences and ramifications of that decision. She thanked her daughter for coming to her with such a difficult decision, and they talked about it at length. She was glad there was a place her daughter felt safe to talk to her.

Another form of communication is to write your children notes. You can do this on special occasions or just whenever to remind them how proud you are of them. Praise is powerful and can help build their self-esteem. They want and need your praise.

One parent had a special ritual when she talked to her teenage son. It was difficult to always meet for dinner as a family when he got into sports, because practices and games got in the way, so she made a special ritual of having "tea and talking" with him. This is particularly important in high school when you can lose your children to friends, work, and school. You need this time to connect. Make rituals of times when you connect with your children.

Allison Merkle Alison

Setting Reasonable Expectations and Sticking to Them

Children need clear expectations during the teenage years. They need limits, curfews, and consequences. Be sure to clearly state them and back them up. Even if your children say "I hate you" for doing this, stay the course, don't lose it, and know that you can't be their friend now. They need a parent. It can be difficult and hard to hear, but they need you to set limits and not put them in a situation they are not yet ready to deal with.

You need to set expectations. This allows your child to know how to act and will help you avoid unnecessary confrontations. For example, when your children are little and you are going to a restaurant or store, talk to them about how you expect them to act before you go in. Also, let them know the consequences if they do not behave correctly. Whatever consequences you set up, you *must* follow through with them when the time comes, or your word means nothing. You need to have a backbone, or your children will run amuck. If you always follow through, they will know that you mean what you say. If you threaten to leave the store if they misbehave, you must leave the store when the time comes. You have to be willing to leave your cart full of groceries and walk out. The good news is it usually only takes one or two times of doing this, and your children will never questions that you are going to follow through on what you said you would do.

You must have reasonable expectations for your children based on their age and ability. Asking a two-year-old to sit quietly for an hour at a restaurant is unreasonable. Instead, you have to take some responsibility and bring toys or things to entertain them during dinner. You don't want to have expectations that inevitably make them fail. This will only discourage them. Don't expect anything they cannot do.

You will have to remind them of your expectations again and again. Gently remind them when they are doing something wrong and explain what is wrong and what you expect. Let them know that the expectations you have for them when you are around are the same when they are with other people. Also, when they do what you expect of them, you can reward their good behavior in some way. This gives your children positive reinforcement to behave well.

Expectations that are positive and reasonable help your children rise to their highest potential. Even if they struggle with something, do not focus on their inability. By focusing on their deficiency, you can create a self-fulfilling prophecy. Encourage them to rise above obstacles with words of praise and in a loving way. If you don't expect better for your children, they won't become the best they can be.

Expectations about school and education are crucial in the early years of your child's life. Having a positive attitude about learning and school, even if it did not go well for you, will help your child be more successful in school. At a young age, talk about the possibility and expectations of college. If you begin this conversation at a young age, your child will grow up thinking it is a given, like high school. Remember to keep your expectations reasonable. If your child gets a B on his report card, don't say, "Why didn't you get an A?" Instead, ask him if he did his best. Did he try his hardest? If he says he did try his hardest, let it go. Doing your best is a reasonable expectation, but expecting an A in everything may be unreasonable for your child. But set clear expectations that homework always gets done on time and that tests should always be studied for.

If your child does something to disappoint you, talk to her about it and help her come up with solutions on how to do better next time. Tell her you know she can do better next time. Always be clear that you love her but don't like the behavior. By helping her come up with a solution, you are letting her feel she has some control over her life. If you always say, "Do it my way or else," your children may rebel. There are some expectations, though, that are nonnegotiable for their own safety, like don't run out in the street. Sometimes, it is just your way.

You must also set expectations. One of the best stories about expectations I ever heard was about a mom taking her children on vacation. I heard this story from a friend, but I wonder if it is a parental myth or a true story. Either way, it is a great story.

This mother was taking her children to see their grandparents who lived very far away. They were going to drive to their grandparents' house, and the children would be in the car together for a very long time, like they were deserted on an island. The mother was terribly distressed about this, because her children often fought in the car. It was bearable for short distances but not for this long drive. So, she came up with a plan. She told them that they were leaving on the trip the day before they were actually supposed to leave. She pretended to put filled suitcases in the car on the day before and put them all in the car like this was the true day. She looked at them before they left the driveway and said, "I expect you to behave on this very long ride. If I hear fighting among you, I will turn the car around and go home."

Well, as expected, they had not gone far, and the children began bickering. She immediately turned the car around and went home without a word. The children were shocked—eyes wide and mouths hanging open. They never believed she would turn around. When they got home, the mother took the suitcases out of the car and went inside. The children came to her, apologized, and begged her to take them to see their beloved grandparents. She told them she would give them one more chance the next day, but that would be it. Her plan worked, and they did not fight the entire trip or on the way back. Sometimes you have to get a little creative as a parent, as illustrated by this story.

Expectations are very important. Children rise to the expectations set for them. As with my own upbringing, my children were raised that college was never "if I go" but "where will I go." There is a college for everyone. But to have an expectation that your child must go to an Ivy League school may be an unreasonable expectation. If you make unreasonable expectations, they feel deflated, like a balloon with no air. Once again, it is an example that parenting is a fine balance.

As a teacher, I hear children who constantly say, "I don't feel good enough" or "No matter what I do it is not enough for my parents." I can't tell you the number of times I have looked a child in the eyes and said, "You are good enough." It is a powerful statement that always brings tears to their eyes. They need to hear from you, not only that they are good enough but that they are awesome and that you are proud of them. Remember, if you set expectations that are too high, your children won't feel good enough.

Keeping Communication Healthy

Screaming at your children is not an effective form of communication. Yes, it may get their attention for the moment, but chances are they won't even remember what you said. If you scream at them in public or in front of friends, chances are they will feel humiliated and resent you. If you are trying to get a point across or teach a lesson, screaming at them about it will not work. Wait until you have calmed down and discuss the issue rationally. We all lose it every once in awhile, but this is not how you communicate. If this is the way you communicate with your children on a regular basis, you need to get help to change this. This is bullying, and you may be creating a bully through your actions.

One of my students told me that in his family the only form of communication they have is screaming. It really bothers him and makes him feel scared. He says no one in the family can really talk to each other rationally, so they end up screaming at each other when things bother them. He said in the heat of the moment, his family has said some awful things to each other. If this is how your family communicates, you need to get help. This is not healthy for you or your children.

Everyone loses it occasionally, but it should be the exception rather than the rule. There are some things you are never allowed to say to your child, even though you may think them in your head. For example, when your teenage daughter is acting like a b****, you cannot say that out loud. Saying, "I hate you," is another example. Don't say something in the heat of the moment, because you can't take back. You can apologize later, but you can't undo the damage. One parent remembers calling her teenage daughter the *B* word. Her daughter is grown but still vividly remembers that conversation and reminds her of it. She really wishes she had not said it, because she can't take it back.

Whatever you put out you get back. So if you put out loving messages to your children, you will hear them when they get older. However, if you say things like, "I hate you," you will hear that back too. "I hate you" was not a phrase I said to my children or one I would tolerate them saying to anyone else; thus, my children never said it to me. They will mimic your words.

To illustrate, when my then-young daughter was misbehaving, I would say to her, "That is inappropriate behavior." I continually said it when she misbehaved, so I was not surprised when she said to a child who was bothering her on the playground one day, "That is inappropriate behavior." Imagine this little four-year-old offering these very grown-up words to another child in the park. I had to laugh when I heard her say it, but I was so glad that was what she said to him in front of all those adults. Be careful what you continually say to your child, because they will repeat it in front of others at some time, even the cuss words you use.

One phrase that really bothered me when my children interacted with each other and that I did not tolerate was "shut up." To me, it sounds harsh and cruel, like a punch in the stomach. I always corrected them and told them they could say "be quiet" but not "shut up." As a teacher, I also correct students when they use phrases like "That is so gay." I feel this is a putdown and could be taken negatively by any of my students possibly struggling with this issue. Remember, they learn their words and values through your words and actions, so if you make comments about gay people, overweight people, minorities, or anyone who is different than you, you are teaching your children to do the same. Your children are like little parrots mimicking you, just like my daughter on the playground so many years ago.

Learning How to Listen

Listening to your children is one of the keys to effective parenting. One of the greatest things I have learned as a teacher is to be a better listener. Looking back on my life, I really wasn't a good listener. When other people were talking, I had a bad habit of not really listening fully and thinking in my head what I would say next. I was so busy formulating what I was going to say when they stopped talking that I really did not hear what they had to say. I was not an active listener.

While teaching for the past ten years, I also sponsored a class called PEER. PEER is an organization at schools that trains students in the school to listen and help other students out. It is an alternative to a guidance counselor if a student doesn't feel comfortable talking to an adult. PEER is associated with the Department of Social Services, and we work with social workers. One of the great things about the program is that the social worker assigned to the school helps train the students on listening skills. Over the years, I have learned so much from this training. I have learned to be an active listener, and it has made me a much better parent, spouse, and friend.

Active listening is actually easy to do. You just have to make a conscious effort to do it. How many times have your children or your spouse come into the room to talk to you while you are busy do something else? You pretend to listen and say "uh huh" a lot, but you are not giving that person your full attention.

In PEER, the students are taught the SOLAR approach to listening. SOLAR stands for Squarely facing the client, Openness of posture (don't have your arms crossed), Leaning forward (slightly), Eye contact, Relaxed. You are showing the person with your body that you are present in the discussion and value them.

We also learned other techniques, such as paraphrasing back what the person said to check for understanding and to make sure you know how they are feeling. For example, "It sounds like you are upset with your teacher because …" We also learned not to pass judgment at all about what the other person tells us. This is hard as a parent when your children come tell you things about their friends. You really have to try to not pass judgment and go crazy when they tell you things. You need to just listen.

When the person is done speaking, the next technique is to use questions that will help him figure out a solution if there is a problem. In PEER, we never give advice; we just help the other person figure out her own solutions. This way, she cannot blame anyone else for the results. This can be a very powerful learning tool for your child. Learning to come up with her own solutions to problems will help her in life. If you are always fixing things for your children, they do not learn to stand on their own two feet. As a parent, I know I still feel the need to impart my wisdom on my own children, and I do from time to time. So next time your child comes to talk to you, stop what you are doing—washing clothes, making dinner, whatever it is—and really listen. Make him feel like he is the most important thing at that moment.

Another one of the lessons I learned in PEER is that children may not be willing to open up to you right away. If you ask, "How are you doing?" the answer is usually "fine." They won't just tell you everything they are feeling when you ask them; this is particularly true with boys. You may have to take them fishing, so to speak. I don't mean literally, but it could be the activity you do to get them talking. What I mean by take them fishing is that you need to do an activity with them, and while you are doing the activity, talk to them. They are more apt to open up to you while doing an activity, because they don't realize they are having a conversation. It can be anything from coloring to actually fishing. Find out what they like to do and do it with them. I even played Guitar Hero through Xbox just to connect with my son. We use this technique in PEER when we mentor the middle school students. We go over to their school twice a month, and we found that we had to do an activity with them to get them talking. Try it. It really works, and it is fun.

By keeping these high standards when it comes to dealing with our children, we keep that constant line of communication open. Our children feel free to express themselves and tell us what is on their minds. Research also supports this fact, showing that in school students felt valued when a teacher listened and cared about them. This was more important to their ability to learn than the teaching itself.

Listen to your children. Let them know that they can always come to you with anything and that you will not judge them or condemn them. Let them know you may not be happy about what they did, but they can always talk to you. As a parent, you can't be too tired or too busy to listen. Even if you are in a situation where one child has needs that require a lot of time, the other children must feel they are important too and that you will listen. They may not come to you 90 percent of the time, but you need to be there for the 10 percent when they do.

Children's hearts are open, and when they know you care about them, they feel loved. Communication comes from your heart, so be there for them and love them by establishing healthy communication habits. If children know they can talk to you, you have done your job as a parent.

Chapter 4 - Discipline and Consequences

> *"All children behave as well as they are treated."*
> *(Anonymous)*

Right around the time my daughter hit the terrible twos, she would get so upset if she did not get her way that her head seemed to spin around as she was screaming, just like in the movie *The Exorcist*. Where had my sweet little girl gone, and what was I going to do about it?

My husband and I were on the same page regarding not wanting to use physical punishment, but we needed to do something—and fast! We read about discipline methods from the experts and watched other parents and decided to try using time-outs. I have to be honest; I was not very good at it at first. But when I finally figured it out, it did work. I literally only had to say, "Do you want to go in time-out?" and she would stop whatever inappropriate behavior she was doing—usually.

I would like to say it worked all the time and forever, but I can't. As she grew older, I had to use new forms of discipline, like taking her phone away or taking away privileges. I also tried to use positive reinforcement and instill respect so she could learn to self-discipline.

What are the secrets of master parents? What do kids really think about discipline? The opinions vary, but one resounding message is clear: fair, loving discipline is an essential part of child rearing.

Why Do Children Need Discipline?

Children need discipline and consequences to learn how to behave. There is a balance to giving love and kindness but also providing boundaries so your children can grow up to be good, law-abiding citizens. You were not given these babies to be friends to them, but rather, you were meant to be a parent to them. When they become functioning adults, then you can be their friend.

We have all seen children who were given very little discipline and grew up to be out-of-control teens and adults. Discipline needs to start when children are young so that it is not a big issue when they are older. Teenagers especially need a strong parent.

Your children may not like the fact you are setting limits and disciplining them at the time, but they will grow up to respect you. In fact, even though parents often feel guilty and like the "bad guy" for disciplining their children, children I have taught make it clear to me that they need parents to teach them right from wrong. Children do ask that parents don't control them completely, though, instead explaining that they need to grow as individuals too.

Methods of Discipline

Whatever your method of discipline, you must differentiate the behavior from the person. Although your child's behavior was bad, he, as a person, is not bad. Tell him, then, that he is not a bad person; he is just making bad decisions.

Some children may take directions easily, while others may need a stern command. Many of us have the tone in our voice that says we mean business when our children push the limits. It can even be used in a quiet way but said in a stern tone. If used infrequently and only at times when you really want to get your children's attention, it can be effective.

There is also "the look." You don't even need to say anything; just give the look. All these methods can be effective if not overused. If used too often, children become desensitized to them. Also, some children literally melt if you raise your voice or give them the look, while others are barely fazed. Children are all different and require different parenting, so it is important to know each of your children well and to find out what methods work best.

Time-out is an effective form of discipline, if done correctly. Time-out is good for both the parent and the child, in fact, because it is a time to separate, breathe, and calm down. In addition, time-out is really a good way for children to learn to calm themselves down or think about what they did to deserve time-out.

Find a place in your house where your children can sit for time-out without any distractions. Some people even have a specific chair called the "naughty chair." When you are first starting time-out with young children, you may need to hold them to teach them what is expected. After they are done in time-out, talk about why they were put there and discuss solutions so it does not happen again.

Sending your children to their rooms for time-out is usually not a good idea, as they may enjoy that. If, however, you do send them to their rooms and believe it is a proper environment for time-out, give them a goal to reach before they can exit. For example, "When you are ready to talk in a nice voice, you can come out."

Other forms of discipline, especially for older children, could mean taking away something they use often. The television, the computer, video games, the car, and the worst for most teenagers, the phone, are great examples of privileges that could be taken away.

One of the most effective discipline techniques, if used sparingly, is the "we are so disappointed" speech. Children really do want you to be proud of them. They don't like disappointing you. But if you are a parent who makes your children feel like this all the time, it will have no effect and probably make them rebel more. What do they have to lose? If, however, you build your children up, they won't want to disappoint you. Give them praise and watch them blossom.

As the saying goes, the punishment should fit the crime. Don't ground children for getting bad grades. Find out what the issue is and try to figure out why their grades are low. Is it lack of dedication and work ethic, or are they struggling and need help? You don't want to make the mistake of punishing your children if they are struggling. Instead, you need to get them help. If they are misbehaving at school, see if there is a reason. Many children act out in school because they are struggling and feel stupid. Make your punishments fit the crime and, moreover, choose punishments that make sense and are not random in nature. For example, if they are late coming home one night, they don't get to go out the next night.

Parenting at Our Best

There are also several things you should never deprive your children of as punishments. You should not tell children that if they misbehave they will not see their loved ones, especially their mother or father. Also, just about every child has that special stuffed animal or blanket that helps him calm down and makes him feel safe. Don't take this away as punishment. Finally, don't keep your children from attending team sports as punishment, as you may be punishing the entire team. Also, you may end up targeting your child as a troublemaker on the team. One of the parents I interviewed, who is also a coach, felt very strongly about not taking away sports for punishment, as it may be the only thing keeping the child in line. Sports can be a way for children to fit in and feel like they belong. For many students, it is the only reason they go to school, and taking it away can make things worse. Also, the coach may be a good resource to help keep children in line.

One important point to remember is that methods of discipline that are seen as reasonable can become unreasonable if abused. For example, I represented two girls who were brought into court because their stepfather was way too tough on them. He used time-outs, but instead of keeping them in time-out a minute for every year of age, he kept them in time out for hours on end, sometimes all afternoon. The girls were sometimes made to sit at the dining room table for hours. He was in the military and treated them like they were too. Don't take discipline to the extreme as this father did. Instead, remember the balance.

Children are all different, and they may need different methods of discipline. What works for one child may not work for another. Don't get frustrated. Instead, just change your style of parenting and methods of discipline to meet each child's needs.

Allison Merkle Alison

Keeping Communication Healthy as We Discipline

Communicating consequences for offenses is critical when doling out punishments. For example, a parent could offer this ultimatum: "I expect you to clean your room today, or you cannot go to the sleepover tonight." Whatever consequences you make, you must be willing to follow through with them. Don't take away the television for a week if you cannot stick with it. Don't say you will cancel a vacation unless you mean it. Give your children reasonable timeframes to get things accomplished.

When children do things that make us angry and we begin to lose it, we must take a minute and collect ourselves. Never discipline when you are angry and upset, because disciplining in anger will not be effective. If you just scream, they just hear that Mom or Dad is angry. It is scary to children to hear their parents scream at them, and you getting angry and upset does not solve the problem. You have lost control and need to calm down. Especially avoid raising your voice with teenagers, because sometimes they are looking to pull your chain.

One parent I spoke to grew up with a father who screamed so loudly that it terrified her. She described him as verbally abusive. His screaming caused her to feel pure fear. When she became a parent, she began screaming at her children. It was what she knew, but she also knew she did not want to do the same thing to her children. So, she sought professional help to stop screaming at her children. She learned different methods of discipline that helped her be a better parent. There are many books, shows, and professionals available to help you overcome anything. Don't be ashamed to get help. Remember, when you know better, you do better.

When you are butting heads with your children, take a deep breath and remember that you will get through this. Don't take it personally. When you take it too personally and get upset, it only makes matters worse. Instead, try to have a sense of humor through it all. We all lose it from time to time, but it can't be your method of disciplining your child every time. Take a breath and calm down. You will make mistakes too. Forgive yourself and move on. Don't dwell on it; learn from it. Also, don't be afraid to tell your child when you are wrong. This is a good chance for them to learn how to apologize and forgive.

One parent I interviewed relayed a story about her nephew. He was two years old at the time, would not listen to his mom, and was having a tantrum. His mother screamed at him at the top of her lungs, "Nobody loves you when you behave this way." The parent who witnessed the incident was appalled because she felt the message was definitely inappropriate and the way it was delivered was out of control. Remember it is the behavior that is bad, not the children themselves. Your children should know you always love them but that their behavior is wrong. Continue to show them you love them, even if they disappoint you.

If you are a person who shuts down and gives people the cold shoulder when they have done something wrong, you are sending the message that you don't love them. Remember that you need to be sending the following message: "I always love you, but I don't like the behavior." You need to discuss the problem and deal with the situation. By not talking to someone for hours or days, you show that person that you do not value him.

I want to touch a little upon emotional abuse as we consider healthy and unhealthy communication. You can say things to your children that are just as damaging as hitting them, maybe even worse. If you call your children names or put them down, you are killing their spirits. I saw these cases in court, although they were tougher to prove. I couldn't provide pictures of this type of wound.

In another instance of emotional abuse, one of my students came to talk to me about the sadness he felt because his family always screamed at each other. He told me that it got so bad that they cussed at each other and said terrible things. I have had many students through the years repeat similar stories. Emotional abuse is a form of abuse that goes on because the wounds are hidden. If you are doing this to your children, you must get help. Be careful what you say; you can't take it all back, and they will always remember it.

Also, remember the balance in parenting and don't make every mistake seem like it is crucial. Pick your battles. If you continually pick and nag at your children, they will stop caring. Remember to also give them positive feedback when they are behaving correctly instead of just negative feedback when they misbehave. This not only builds up their self-esteem but also teaches them about the behavior you expect. For example, say things like "I really like how you played with your brother today" or "Your behavior at the restaurant was great." This way, they will also know when you are pleased.

The Controversy Surrounding Corporal Punishment

When it comes to using corporal punishment as a means of discipline, I am totally biased in my view due to the years I spent in the child abuse and neglect courts. I cannot even remotely speak to the benefits of spanking. Even the American Academy of Pediatrics recommends, "Parents be encouraged and assisted in the development of methods other than spanking for managing undesired behavior."[v]

I personally don't think it is possible to discipline your child with corporal punishment in a calm, caring manner, although I know there are many parents who feel they can do it. Some of the parents I spoke to felt that parents do not have the right to hit their children and that spanking seems like more of a release for the parents than a teachable moment for the children themselves.

I feel so strongly about this issue because I saw many of the harmful effects of its use. I have seen children who have been beaten with a hand, a brush, an extension cord, a switch, and countless other objects that their parents grabbed in the heat of the moment to use on them. None of this was done in a loving or caring method.

I have also seen well-intentioned parents hit their teenagers with their hands and leave handprints on their faces. I have seen the black-and-blue marks, the cuts, and the emotional damage such punishment inflicts on a child. I even had several parents look at me and say, "I was just doing what my parents had done to me and their parents had done to them. I didn't know it was wrong." My heart literally hurts when I see a parent strike a child in a store or park in the heat of anger. I understand the frustration, but I don't understand the abuse.

One parent I interviewed did spank her child at a young age and hit him so hard she left a handprint on him. She felt horrible and knew that if someone had seen it and reported it to the authorities that she could have had her child taken away. She never spanked him again and used different methods of discipline.

Many of the parents I spoke to were spanked and paddled as children and made a conscious effort not to do this to their children. They wanted to handle their own children more calmly, believing, "If you hit them, they will hit back." Some of them even resented their parents today for hitting them when they were children. Although spanking may seem effective in the moment because it stops the behavior temporarily, it instills a relationship based on fear. It may be a parent's immediate reaction, but it can be abusive and the memories of it never go away.

One parent stated that he was hit as a child and was afraid of his parents even as an adult because of all the years of corporal punishment. Yes, it got his attention as a child, but his lifelong relationship with his parents was one based in fear. He never felt like he had a healthy relationship with his parents. Later, he made a conscious effort not to hit his son, because he did not want his relationship with him based in fear but in love and understanding. He did feel that children needed discipline and consequences, but he was sure there were better, less violent methods.

Instead, he disciplined through time-outs and learned through the Brazelton method, which advises that a child should have a minute in time-out for each year of age.[vi] For example, a two-year-old child should only be in time-out for two minutes, a three-year-old child for three, and so on. It was difficult to break this cycle of hitting, but in the long run he was glad he did it, as he has a much better relationship with his son than he had with his parents.

I also had a case involving several families where the children were taken away because of abuse. They were using corporal punishment because their church insisted they use it. One of the founding principles of this church was that the parents had to beat the children if they misbehaved. The members had their children taken away and had to go to parenting classes to learn better methods of discipline. I remember how shocked some of the parents were, because they felt they were just following the dictates of their church. It was as if it was okay to beat their children just because the church encouraged and even seemed to demand it. Abuse is abuse, even if it is a principle doctrine of your church.

I can remember one time I was with my daughter at the park and a little boy hit another child at the park. The mother of the child who hit the other child went up to him and started hitting him, saying, "Don't hit other children." Can you imagine this picture? It was so ridiculous. The mother was hitting the child for hitting. I wanted to tell her, "He is just doing what you taught him."

Unfortunately, I also saw horrible physical abuse that any reasonable human would consider abuse. There is no way you could even label it discipline. When I was witnessing all this in court, I was a mom of two young children. I was so confused about how to discipline my children properly. One case in particular taught me the greatest lesson on child rearing I ever experienced.

This case is not what you would expect to hear about in the child abuse and neglect court, because the child I represented clearly came from a loving, caring family. These parents were not in court because they did something to their child but because they didn't do something. The case involved a young teenage girl who would sneak out of her bedroom window each night to go hang with gang members. Her uncle was a policeman, and he would hunt her down and bring her home. Her parents finally got so discouraged they actually had her arrested and turned into Social Services.

On the day I was handed her case, she was very remorseful and had even written a letter to her parents apologizing and promising to never do it again. She spoke about how much she loved her parents as the tears streamed down her eyes. I felt her love for her parents and truly believed she was sorry for what she had done. When we went before the judge and reunited her with her parents, it was a love fest. Everyone felt sure she could go home and that the family would get family counseling to deal with the issues. This seemed like an easy case to all of us in the courtroom.

Weeks went by, and I really did not think about the case until one day the case was brought before the court on an unscheduled day. I was confused as to why we were hearing the case, because the family was not due back for six months. The social worker had put the case on the docket to report that my client had once again snuck out of her window in the middle of the night. Only this time she was not coming home. She and another young person had been shot execution style and killed. I still get teary eyed and feel a bit of the same shock I felt that day now. This was a young girl from the valley of California who grew up in suburbia. She had a good family who loved her. How did this happen? I went home and held my two-year-old daughter a little tighter than usual. How would I keep her from climbing out the window when she was a teenager?

I went to her funeral, and at this time, I was about seven months pregnant with my son. I can remember that day like it was yesterday. I had written a card to the parents expressing my deep remorse for not being able to help them. I did not even know if they would want me at her funeral, because I felt as if I had failed her and them. When I arrived at the funeral, I was surprised by the number of people there, particularly teenagers. I sat in the back and listened to people speak about this young lady in a loving and caring way. She had many friends from school. She had been a member of her youth group at church. Her parents seemed to be highly regarded in the community. They stood there so calm and lovingly. I could not wrap my brain around this. How could this happen?

As I was sitting there thinking about it, I had a big "aha" moment. I thought back to my teenage days and knew there was no way I would have ever climbed out my window to go with anyone, let alone gang members. My parents would have killed me. Not literally, of course, but I would have been in serious trouble. Why didn't this young lady feel that way? I will never know all the details of why she did what she did. But what I got out that day was that you must discipline your children and set limits and consequences. You must parent and instill a little healthy fear—no, I am not sure fear is the right word; maybe respect is a better term—so they never climb out the window into danger.

Do not raise your hand to your child. It sends the wrong message. Your physical superiority is not necessary to get your point across. It is demeaning to you and your children, and there are other ways to control your children. If you were physically or emotionally abused as child and are concerned you will repeat the same behavior, get help. There are professional people who can help you break the cycle before you pass it on to your children.

Final Thoughts about Discipline

In the end, no matter what disciplinary methods you choose, make sure you are on the same page as your spouse. Children know how to divide parents, especially when they are determined to get their way. If your spouse takes the phone away and you give it back, your spouse becomes the mean parent. If you are always undermining your spouse, it will detrimentally affect your children's relationship with that parent and your relationship with your spouse. Never say "Wait until your father gets home" for punishment. Consequences need to occur right away. You and your spouse should discuss your views on discipline and consequences when your children are young and try and be united. Even if you disagree from time to time, do it away from your children and try not to undermine each other. This can be particularly difficult and more crucial in divorce situations.

Don't bring anger with you. Don't be mad today about yesterday. Start fresh each day. Don't hang on to negative feelings. Show your children how to get over things and move on. A big thing that influences your children's behavior is your presence in their lives. Be there to show them how to behave.

The moral of the story is this: you must discipline and make consequences. It is our duty to help our children learn to be valuable, productive citizens. But, again, it must be with balance. You should not physically or emotionally abuse your children, but you should parent as best you can with good methods of discipline.

Chapter 5 - Education

"Education is the great engine of personal development. It is through education that the daughter of a peasant can become a doctor, that a son of a mineworker can become the head of the mine, that a child of farm workers can become the president of a nation."[vii] *(Nelson Mandela)*

Today's news is full of stories blasting the education system, and in my experiences as a lawyer, educator, parent, and citizen, I have seen both good and bad schools. To be honest, the good schools are in areas where the communities are involved and take pride in them. It is a community effort.

There are so many schools doing outstanding jobs and teachers working so hard that I sometimes get frustrated over all the bashing that goes on. Can we do better? Of course, we always can. Are there schools in areas that are not meeting the needs of the students? Yes, but one can't just look to the school system to educate his or her children.

Recently, this same point was made by Thomas L. Friedman in his article "How About Better Parents" published in the *New York Times.*

> In recent years, we've been treated to reams of op-ed articles about how we need better teachers in our public schools and, if only the teachers' unions would go away, our kids would score like Singapore's on the big international tests. There's no question that a great teacher can make a huge difference in a student's achievement, and we need to recruit, train and reward more such teachers. But here's what some new studies are also showing: We need better parents. Parents more focused on their children's education can also make a huge difference in a student's achievement.[viii]

This point, one made so passionately by Friedman, is one that is critically important to the successful parents I interviewed as well. As they explained, school is a big part of their children's lives, so parents must play a major role in helping them do well in it instead of just relying on the school or teachers to educate their children. The parents' job, they made clear, is to do everything possible to help their children be successful in life and to show them how to get along in society.

Getting Involved

One of the big questions that comes up is how involved should you be in your children's schools. I had an issue when my daughter was in middle school that brought this issue home to me. She has been placed on a fast track for math in sixth grade. However, her seventh-grade teacher became very ill and could not teach, and she and the students in her classes had different substitutes who did not know the math for the remainder of the school year.

Parenting at Our Best

Throughout this time, my daughter told me she was not learning anything in math. I was concerned about her education, but I also felt bad for the sick teacher. I was relieved when my daughter passed the state-mandated math test and felt things were fine, but the next year she had a tough teacher whom she did not like. This teacher was really hard on her and demanded a lot from her. She began to feel bad about herself, because she was behind in the learning from the year before.

The lack of a good teacher in seventh grade clearly showed itself in eighth grade. For the first time in her life, she was not enjoying math. I did get involved and talked to the teacher, and I found out my daughter was not completing all her assignments on time. This was unacceptable to me. It is one thing to struggle when you are trying your best and doing all your work on time, but it is another to not be doing the work at all. It was like she was really shutting down and disliking math.

After finding out she was not turning in her work on time, my husband and I took her phone and computer away until she got her math grade back up. This was tough love, as both of those things were her lifelines. Needless to say, she was not happy with us. However, she quickly improved her efforts and at the end of the year did pass the state-mandated test again.

I was concerned, though, that she had not really learned the math well and that it would affect her performance in high school math classes as well. As many of us know, math is a subject that builds on itself, and students really need to learn as they go or it becomes tough to progress and succeed. I did not want her to keep feeling behind and frustrated, so I took her off the fast track and had her repeat the math she had just taken in her freshman year.

That was the best decision I could have made, as she is now doing fine in all her high school math classes. When I look back at the entire situation, I realize I should have gotten involved in seventh grade and made sure she was getting the education she needed. If I had to do it over again, I would have contacted the principal to make sure a proper substitute was found.

This story illustrates an important point: you need to be active in your children's schools. You need to make sure they are getting a good education. Make sure the schools they attend are good ones. You can check out your schools online to see how well they help students pass state tests and how many go on to college. Look at the size of classes to see how crowded they are. What extracurricular opportunities do the schools provide? What types of support are available for struggling students?

In elementary school, you should be more involved than in middle and high school levels. The idea is that in elementary school you help your children develop good study habits; in middle school you are still involved but are starting to give them more responsibility; and by high school they should be doing it on their own, meeting or exceeding goals, and earning successful marks. Remember that you need to help your children become self-sufficient so when they go off to college they will be successful. Keep in mind, though, every child is different, and some children will require more guidance than others. But the end goal is always the same: help them develop habits that will make them self-sufficient.

Another important way you can help your children through the school years is to be supportive of your children and listen when they have concerns about school or a teacher. They may just need to vent and do not need you to fix anything; talking may help them relieve stress.

If you have real concerns, talk to the teacher and see if that alleviates any worries you or your children may have. Developing a good relationship with your children's teachers will help you be more comfortable asking questions and having tough conversations. Let the teachers know you care and will support your children's learning. Don't just put it all on the teachers; parents also need to help their children be successful. If you continue to be concerned, talk to the guidance counselor or an administrator. Remember, though, don't automatically judge a teacher based on rumors; find out for yourself.

Remember too that some of the best teachers are seen as tough at first but then the children come to love them. Also, it is inevitable that at some time in our children's school experiences, they will get a teacher they do not like. When this occurs, don't be so quick to rush in and fix the situation. Your children should be taught to respect teachers, no matter if they like them or not. It's important not to allow teacher bashing to go on, or it could lead to disrespect issues at school. Instead, tell your children that someday they may have a boss they don't like, but they have to be successful despite them. Teaching your children to be successful despite the teacher will help them handle any situation.

Children learn differently, so they may need additional accommodations to meet their full potential. If your children do need additional services in school, work with the teachers and staff respectfully. It is important to be your children's advocate and to make sure they get the services they need, but you must do so respectfully. If your children require special services and become part of the special education department, don't be afraid of them being labeled in some way. Many children benefit from the services offered and go on to college and the workforce become very successful. The main focus should be about getting them the help they need to be and feel successful in school, so ask early and get help for your children if needed.

One parent's child was struggling in kindergarten, and her pediatrician helped her get him professionally tested, which local schools may be able to facilitate also. The pediatrician told her, "He will get through school, but let's make sure he gets an education."

The doctor found he had a high IQ but had ADD (attention deficit disorder), and they were able to work out a plan for him. The boy went on to become a doctor. If they had not had him tested and realized what was going on, he may have struggled all through school and been labeled things like lazy, disruptive, or lacking in some way when in truth he just learned differently.

Even if you are involved with your children's development and learning, children do learn differently, and it is up to parents to find solutions that work, even if that means supplementing your children's education at home. To illustrate, I remember when my son was young and the kindergarten teacher told me she was a little concerned about him moving on to first grade because of his limited vocabulary skills. I had worked with him and taught him at an early age, the same as my older daughter who had performed just fine in school, so I wondered what the problem could be.

The teacher gave me suggestions and ideas on how I could work with him over the summer to try and catch him up, preparing him for the year ahead. Of course, I was a little freaked out and took this on as a top priority, so over the summer, we worked on flashcards and read even more than we already did. I did not want him to end up disliking learning, so I was careful to make it fun and acted like it was no big deal. I even used positive incentives to get him to work with me.

When I went to the first conference with his first-grade teacher at the beginning of the year, I mentioned all we had done that summer. She was surprised he had been behind since he was doing so well. She did not even know there had been an issue.

I learned a valuable lesson from this experience with my son: children do learn at different paces, but we can and should help them so they can be successful in school. If your children are struggling, help them. If you can't do it, get professional help. What is funny about the lesson I learned is that my son remembers that summer in a fond way still today.

The experiences children have in the younger years set them up for the rest of their education. Just think about it; people do not like to do something they are not good at. You have to help them be good at it. Don't rely on the teacher or school to do this.

Many children do well in school because they want to make their parents proud, so building a positive relationship will help them be successful. If they start having success in school early on, they will experience how good it feels to do well and will continue building on this success. If your children struggle at a young age, get them the help they need so they don't get so discouraged they end up dreading school. If they aren't successful, they will dislike it. Help them have little successes, and you can build on that and try to make it a positive experience.

Teaching Communication and Reading Skills

One of the biggest things parents can do to help their children be successful in school is to talk to them so they develop good communication skills, as discussed earlier in our chapter on communication. Talk to them as babies, even though they may not understand. Introduce new words to them so their vocabulary can grow. Instead of always saying, "Are you hungry?" try saying, "Are you famished?"

Encourage them to learn through play also. For example, help them play with puzzles or building blocks when they are old enough to do so. These can help children develop critical thinking skills. Completing a puzzle on their own can give them a sense of accomplishment. You could also have them learn music by singing or playing instruments. There are many educational toys that help encourage development and learning as well. Playing games can help their brains develop, and using flashcards for fun can help them read.

Try to make a learning game out of everyday tasks. When you are shopping, make a game of counting things. Math skill can be developed by such simple daily games. When you are driving in the car, play games like the license plate game to encourage reading. If you are not familiar with this game, one plays by using the alphabet; have your child look for license plates containing each letter of the alphabet. Begin by finding an *A*, and then proceed to move through the entire alphabet.

Also, have your children attend a preschool program before entering kindergarten to get them ready for the demands of attending school regularly. This helps them learn some social skills and gets them used to being away from you. One of the great programs offered by our government is Head Start. It is a program that helps children in poverty receive educational experiences before they are sent to kindergarten. It helps them get a head start in life, thus the name. In short, during these early years, expose your children to as many new things as possible to expand their knowledge base.

Another important goal for parents is to help develop a love for reading in their children. It is critical to read to your children when they are infants and throughout their childhood, because reading is important in every subject they will encounter throughout their school years and will determine much of their success when they are adults. If your children are good readers, it will help them do well in school and on standardized tests like the SATs.

Make reading a nightly ritual from birth. Reading at night can be a special time with your children, and reading out loud helps build your children's vocabulary. Even when they are older, you can continue reading out loud by taking turns doing it. You can even do funny voices for each character to make it more fun.

Even though first grade seems to be the year most children begin to read, each child is different. Some may start earlier, and some may not pick it up until later. Don't worry about when it happens; be concerned about instilling a love for it. One parent with five children became nervous when one of his sons did not read by first grade. He worked with him with flashcards, read out loud with him, and used many other techniques, and then one day it just clicked and his son started reading. Be active in their lives and help them.

Also, take your children to the library and make it a special treat to get a library card. Give books as special gifts that your children will cherish. Have more books than toys in your house. If your children see you and your spouse reading, this also encourages them. Many parents read the same books as their adolescent children and then talk about the book with them. They try to guess what was going to happen next. They go see the movies of any of the books they read, like the Harry Potter and Twilight series. If you are driving a long distance in the car, instead of always popping in a video, listen to books on tape. Do whatever you can to get your children excited about reading.

Instilling a Love of Learning

Another important thing you can do to help them be successful is to inspire a love of learning, because you want to make sure your children are interested and love school. Take an interest in what your children are learning. If you value education, then your children will too, so make it a priority.

One parent I interviewed who did not do well in school when he was young decided he would be a part of his child's education and encourage education with his son. His son went on to become a high achiever in school all because the father changed his own attitude about education and got involved.

Another parent who was a guidance counselor said it was very common to hear in meetings with parents, "Oh yeah, I did not do well in school either" or "I didn't like school myself." Even if you did feel that way, stop yourself from passing that view on to your children and encourage a love of learning instead. It will help them be more successful in school.

Some parents showed their love for learning by being role models and taking classes or getting their master's degrees. Their children saw firsthand the passion and dedication they had about education. Remember, even if you did not like school, you can still teach your children to have a love for education so they can be successful. Talk to them about what it takes to be successful and about the importance of hard work.

Another way you can inspire a love for learning is through hands-on experience. Go to museums and participate in historical reenactments. One parent talked about the fact that his parents did not have a lot of money but educated his brothers and sisters by taking them camping throughout the United States. He really appreciated learning about each state and it built great memories with his family.

Another parent who had two children, both valedictorians of their classes, made learning a priory by having "adventure days." Once or twice a week and all through summer vacations they visited museums and took trips to historical locations. There are unusual and interesting museums all over the place. This parent exposed her children to new things and created a spark for learning.

Another idea this parent utilized was supplementing core learning in school. If her child was learning about a particular subject or event at school, she worked hard to supplement this learning on her own. For example, they watched the Discovery Channel together and made learning new things exciting. She related this type of parenting to a parent that helps his or her child be successful in a sport. Just like that child focuses on a sport, they focused on learning. Her children were not the superstars on the athletic field, but they were the superstars in the classroom. She really went out of her way to instill this love for learning in her children, and it paid off.

Setting Up Household Routines

Make sure your children get a good night's sleep and a nutritional breakfast before you send them off to school each day. Even when they are teenagers, try to make sure they get sleep, because sleep is essential to good mental function. Make sure mornings are a calm and enjoyable experience so they can go to school on a positive note and start the day right too. If your mornings are stressful, your children bring that stress to school, and it can negatively affect their day.

Also teach them how to be organized. When they get into school, teach them how to use their school agenda to plan out what things are due each day. You can also provide them with a big calendar or whiteboard to map out their work. Teaching this skill early on will help them in high school and college. Also, explain to them the importance of being organized and teach them methods to do so.

Limit screen time. That means you should limit the computer, television, and phone so that they have time to get their homework done and study for tests. Limiting screen time also gets your children interacting with people. Only allow them on video games for a certain amount of time a day. Many parents I interviewed would not allow their children to go on the Internet unsupervised and had a family computer out in the open. Some parents did not let their children watch television during the week and only on the weekend in the hope of promoting other activities. Many did not allow televisions in their children's bedrooms. Also, make sure to remove gadgets and screen access when it is homework time.

Set up a homework routine early, so your children get used to a regular schedule that includes homework. If someone else watches your children, make sure they have a routine set up as well. This regular routine will help your children get things done and feel successful in school. Teaching them a routine will also teach them time management skills.

Many of us, including many of the parents I interviewed, feel that children should come home from school, have a snack, and get their homework done before they go out and play. This is vital to instill the message that getting work done before playtime is important.

Teach your children how to do their homework and be there if they need help. Also teach them how to study for a test. As a teacher, one of the biggest disconnects I see with students is how to study. We always say to them "go study" or "make sure you study for that test tonight," but I really don't think a lot of students have ever learned what that means or how to do it.

I remember seeing one of my advanced placement history students about thirty minutes before school started in the library on the day of a big test we were having. The next day he came to talk to me because he did not do well on the test. When I talked to him about it, he seemed a little indignant and said, "I should have done better. I came in that morning to study."

I started questioning him about his studying and what I realized was his idea of studying and my idea of studying were two very different things. To him, he had studied just because he went to the library the morning of the test. To him, studying meant twenty minutes in the library looking over some things.

I asked him some questions about the information we were studying to see if he knew the basic information, and he could not even tell me definitions of simple terms. I looked at him and explained very simplistically that studying entails looking over the information until you know it very well. He looked at me like I was crazy. "No," I said, "that is what the students who do well do." He replied matter-of-factly, "Oh no, those kids are just smart." He could not grasp the idea that "those kids" knew the material well and knew what it meant to study.

Since that day, I really try as a teacher to teach study skills and get the message across that if you want to do well on a test, you must know the information really well. There is still such a disconnect with many of the students I teach. Some use the excuse, "I am just not a good test taker." My response is, "No, you just have not learned the best ways for you to study."

There are many ways to help your children learn to study early on. It is up to you as their parent to teach them these skills, even if you did not know them already. Some examples to teach your children to study are to have them outline the chapters in the book to make a study tool, or they could also make note cards of the important terms to study from. You could go on the Internet and go on websites like Quizlet to make note cards and play learning games. They could complete supplemental work you assign, and you could even quiz them on the information after they claim to have studied. In short, there are many methods to help children learn how to study; just know you have to play an active role in their education to help them be successful.

During summer vacation, continue learning by practicing math and reading and by learning about new things. There are many summer programs at libraries that could help you out. There are also camps designed for learning. It is important to keep kids' minds involved to keep them sharp for the challenges they will face during the next school year.

In the end, don't ever say homework is a waste of time or stupid even if you feel this way, and certainly don't let this attitude be a household philosophy. Your children will pick up on this and use it as an excuse, and they will also use it as a reason to procrastinate.

One parent talked about an experience with his daughter in middle school where she waited until the last minute to do a major project she was dreading. It was very stressful on the family dealing with her trying to get it done at the last minute. He used that experience as a lesson to teach the dangers of procrastination. He told her, "I don't want to have to revisit this situation again. You need to do things on time and learn to budget your time."

If you set up good study habits young, you may not have to be so involved in middle and high school. It will be routine to them.

Setting Reasonable Goals

Setting goals that make education relevant can help your children want to achieve in school. If your children playact doctor or teacher when they are little, tell them that they too can become those things one day if they work hard in school. Talk about college at a young age so that it is a given when they graduate high school. Tell them how much fun college is and, in the process, teach them how important it is to have a goal to work toward in school.

Another thing you can do to help your children be successful in the future is to try and discover their passions and steer them to a related profession. I see students struggling in school and having no motivation because they have no goals or dreams. Having goals gives children the reason to do well in school, even if they change those goals several times. Even having the generic goal of going to college can help. This helps them have a desire to work hard in school.

Talk to your children about their goals and maybe even help them figure them out by writing things down. Remember that none of this is set in stone. You will get many calls from your children in college telling you they have changed their major. In fact, it is reported that the average student who enters college with a declared major changes it three to five times before they graduate.[ix] However, having a goal to attain helps children realize the importance and significance of doing well in school, even if they later decide to change that goal.

There are some children, though, that despite their parents' encouragement, fight about going to college. They go through a particularly rebellious time and talk about wandering through Europe or getting a job. Try hard to encourage them to go to college, but at some point, you may have to resign yourself to the fact that some children take different paths in life than what we plan for them. One parent talked about her rebellious teenager who refused to go to college right out of high school and later, on her own, went on to become an attorney. Remind your children that if they do well in high school, they will have more options in college choices.

Remember through the school years to not demand perfection, as this can lead to frustration and dislike for school. If you demand perfection, you will create problems. Ask them and expect them to do their best. Do be clear on your expectations, but don't create a bad situation by demanding too much. Another parent, who was also a teacher, witnessed many cases when students would sabotage their education just to get back at a parent who expected too much. They would purposefully not do their work to assert some control in their lives, knowing they would never please their parents no matter what they did.

Motivating Your Children to Succeed in School

There is a lot you can do to help your children be successful in school. You play a crucial role in this, so don't just sit back and expect the teachers or school to do it all.

Remember, your children's "job" when they are young adults is school. That should be their focus. Being involved in extracurricular activities is a good thing to help get into college, but school must come first. Never let "I couldn't get my homework done because I had practice" be an excuse. If your children are going to be involved in activities, they must learn to balance their time. Also remember to support them in school and all their school activities by showing up to all their events.

Motivation to do well should come from within so that as they get older they work hard because they want to be successful. Many parents do not believe in paying for grades, and some other parents reward their children with monetary rewards for high grades. For some children, this may be their only motivation to do well, but motivation should come from within. Also, how do you put a value on a grade? How much is enough? When they are teenagers, no amount of money may be enough.

Although my husband and I did not pay for grades, we did go out to special dinners or get ice cream to celebrate our children's successes. We also created learning opportunities when our kids earned lower grades. For example, my son still reminds me of the time in sixth grade when he brought home his first C; I made him watch a documentary on terrible jobs like digging ditches. I may have gone a little overboard, but I wanted him to get the bigger point.

My husband and I agree that verbal praise is not only important but probably the most effective. Tell your children you are proud of them; they need to hear it. Also display the work they do at school to show them how proud you are of them.

In the end, I often tell my students that they don't need to play the lottery to win big. Their lottery winning is their education. If they work hard in school, doors will open up for them and they well have many more choices in life. Education is the true equalizer.

When I worked in the court system with troubled teens, it was clear that many of them had no motivation to do well in school at all. In fact, if you asked me one of the common factors in the students I saw locked up, one would be being unsuccessful in school. That is one reason it is so important to help your children be successful in school and help them develop a love of learning. Education gives them a step up in the world and helps them be all they can be. I have watched children come from nothing and rise up through education, so imagine what your children will be able to do with your help, support, and encouragement.

Chapter 6 - Family Time, Dinner, and the Extended Family

"Each day of our lives we make deposits in the memory banks of our children."[x] *(Charles R. Swindoll)*

As an attorney, nothing was more heartbreaking than when I watched children in court have absolutely no family members present at their hearings. They literally had no one in their lives that cared enough to be present. I can't imagine how it feels to be in a courtroom as they were, so scared and so alone. Is it any wonder that a significant amount of foster children end up in jail or prison when they become adults?[xi] Or is it little surprise that children of incarcerated parents are likely to become incarcerated too? [xii]

We need our families to help us grow. Whether that family is a mother, father, and children or some other form of family, we all need to belong. I watched many young people turn to gangs in the streets of Los Angeles because it gave them the sense of family they were so desperately seeking. Although these are extreme situations, your children need that connection too. Don't think that working so hard to provide for your children financially makes up for your absence. They need you present in their lives, just like the foster children and children whose parents are incarcerated need theirs.

Making Family Time Sacred

According to the parents I interviewed and my own experiences, family time is critical to children's development, because it is gives them a sense of belonging. Even simple activities like hiking or going to the movies as a family can be fun.

Family time does not have to cost money. You can do things that are inexpensive or even free, like riding bikes, taking walks, or playing games. Your children want to spend time with you. It is not always about the material things you can provide for them.

Sometimes you may have to require family time, particularly during the early teen years. Don't just allow your children to be in their rooms all day, as if they were strangers renting rooms in your house. Make it mandatory to spend some time with the family. Eventually, they will come around; you may even be surprised when they ask for family time themselves at some point. What you give out, you will get back when they are older.

One parent I interviewed who came from a family of nine talked about how her friend envied her for having the family time she had as a child; her friend wished she'd had that meaningful time with her family. The friend told her she was lucky that her parents made that time.

Religion is an important avenue that gives families opportunities to spend time together. People are so busy that Sunday Mass may be the only time the family is together all week. No specific religion is better than another. Many of us feel that religion also teaches children important values and gives them guidance—for example, learning little things like the importance of being kind to others. Many religious values have been passed down from generation to generation. As the saying goes, a family that prays together stays together. Also, consider that faith and belief can bring comfort to a child.

Vacations as a family are another way to build family ties. One parent talked about the fact that her family went to the beach each summer as a family. There was no television or friends distracting the kids, so they hung out with the family playing games. For another parent, vacations were important to take with her children because her parents never took them when she was a child. Her dad worked all the time and wasn't around. She wanted to make sure her children had the memories that she never got herself.

When it comes to vacations, don't let the early teen years stop you from continuing your traditional vacations. Although they may complain about them and the time missed with friends, this is the time period your children need family time more than ever.

Giving your children chores can also be a way to encourage a strong family and to teach children self-worth and self-satisfaction. Assigning chores sends the message that we all help each other out because we are a part of a family. One parent talked about the fun he has with his children when they are doing the chores together. He jokes around with them and appreciates that time, even if it is work.

Some parents I interviewed felt they should not have to pay their children for chores, as the work is their responsibility as a member of the family, while others thought it was important to give an allowance to teach financial responsibility. Many of the students I have come to know through teaching clarify that making them work for things they want through the completion of chores gives them a sense of accomplishment and a reminder that they are part of the family. Don't do everything for them, they urge, but also have balance and don't make them do everything. They also advise not to take it too far and give them so many chores that they don't feel taken care of.

Family time can be supporting each other in personal and extracurricular interests too. For example, having siblings attend each other's games can foster close sibling relationships. No matter what activities you choose, make time for family when your children are young so they value it when they are older.

All these experiences are opportunities for you to spend time with your children and teach them your values. Building this connection with your children will really help you when you go through the tough times. You are giving them the foundation to get through anything life throws at them. They always know they have their family in their lives no matter what. Having that family support is essential, and it gives children stability knowing there are people who are always there for them. It sends the message that the family looks after each other and its members are a part of something special.

Dinnertime

Dinner is one of the best ways to connect with your family each day. It may be the one time in the day you actually check in with each other and communicate. It is such an important ritual in a child's life. At dinner, you get the chance to see how each person's day went. If you are unable to have dinner each night as a family due to your job or other commitments like sports teams, you can still make Sunday dinner or breakfast the special time. Even if one parent cannot be present at dinnertime, still come together as a family and eat together. This ritual really helps out in the teenage years when children's lives get so busy with school and friends. It may be the one chance to still connect with them during these busy teen years. For some older children, it may also be the only time you can guarantee they get a nutritional meal.

You can make dinner fun by having all members say something they were grateful for in their day or by playing simple games like "I spy" or doing math problems. No matter what you talk about or do during dinnertime, create a tradition that makes your children feel valued and safe. Don't have dinner in front of the television, as it will get in the way of the time to connect. Don't allow cell phones either. By limiting outside interferences, it shows that your time together is important and that you care.

According to my many students, dinnertime as a family is often the one constant thing in their lives. They can picture the kitchen table vividly, and they know how it feels to be part of it the regular family dining there. Missing a dinner or two a week together is not so bad, they explain, because as they get older it can get tough to always sit down to dinner with their hectic schedules and commitments to activities. Some of them even go a day without talking to their parents, they explain. However, many students explain how they miss dinnertime when it does not occur regularly, because it is their chance to talk and connect. One foreign exchange student I spoke to learned the value of dinnertime through his host family. At home in his country, both his parents worked and were too busy to do sit down for a meal together.

The importance of dinnertime was really driven home to me my first year teaching high school. The subject of dinner came up during one of our discussions in government class, and I was surprised to learn of so many students who did not have dinner with their families. In fact, about half the class said they did not come together as a family for dinner. One student said that his mother did make dinner each night, but instead of eating together, they each came and took their meals to separate rooms. He seemed a little sad that he did not have this ritual. He said he would go for days and not talk to his parents; it was like they were strangers living under one roof. The students who did eat dinner with their families were very proud of the fact they had this time together and boasted of rich dinner tales anecdotes.

My absolute favorite times are when I get to have all my children and husband home for dinner. This was an important part of my daily ritual growing up, and I continued it with my family. Dinner is the one ritual I try very hard to make sure happens as often as possible. The big joke in our family is that my son takes so long to eat just so we can stay with each other at dinner longer. I absolutely love sitting around the table talking to them, and those are the moments when I know I am so blessed.

In fact, according to a *Time* magazine article in 2006, "Studies show that the more often families eat together, the less likely kids are to smoke, drink, do drugs, get depressed, develop eating disorders and consider suicide, and the more likely they are to do well in school, delay having sex, eat their vegetables, learn big words and know which fork to use."[xiii] The benefits are endless. It is not just about the meal; it is about the connections that occur.

There may be times when there are conflicts at dinner over an issue, but don't let that stop this important connecting time. Dinner is a time to really listen to your children and show them you value them. Many of us know the importance of dinner to children, because we often have stray children at our dinner tables with us. They don't even mind eating the vegetables, unlike our own children, as they are so clearly happy to be a part of the experience. Some children never get that connection because their families eat their meals in separate rooms.

Be careful not to make dinner a negative time. With the obesity issue at an all time high, gone are the days where you should make you children eat everything on their plates. They should learn to eat until they are full. To get them to eat their vegetables, just encourage them to eat a least some of them. Making them sit at the table until they eat everything on the plates is not only unhealthy but makes dinnertime stressful.

Also, make one dinner that everyone eats. Start this at a young age so they learn to try new things. I knew of a parent who made different meals for each of her children because they did not like certain foods. They became very picky eaters, and she was a stressed out mother. If you start the habit of making only one meal each night and expecting your children to eat most of it, you will not have this issue. You can still take turns making certain dinners on different nights that each child likes.

Creating and Keeping Family Traditions

Creating family traditions is another essential way to make connections with your children. One of my favorite traditions besides the usual holiday traditions is one we do on Valentine's Day. I got the idea from my hairstylist when my children were young. On Valentine's Day every year, my husband and I would blow up as many red, pink, and white balloons as we could and put them in the playroom. My cheeks hurt thinking about it. My children would wake up to a balloon fest of fun, and we would spend hours playing in them. We would laugh so hard our stomachs hurt, and the memories were priceless. Even today, I still send them the balloons in care packages in college. The message on this special day was and still is "I love you." They didn't need a Valentine; we celebrated through our own tradition.

Building traditions in your family is a priceless way of bonding the members together. For example, you can start a tradition of building gingerbread houses over the holidays each year or having fondue night once a month. You can go to the pumpkin patch each fall or go to see the Easter Bunny every Easter. Go see holiday lights during the season and make special dinners for each holiday. The traditions you build could be based on your preserving your culture or ones you create for fun. You can also build traditions that just the nuclear family participates in. For example, you can always celebrate a certain holiday together and save other ones for the extended family and friends.

One family built a tradition that when there were big family decisions to make, they all went to Pizza Hut and had dinner. While they were there, they discussed the family issue and worked it out together. Another family also used pizza as their tradition by making Fridays family pizza night. On these nights, they watched a movie or played games together.

Have specific traditions for each child. In a big family, it can be hard for children to get some one-on-one time with a parent. One parent made fishing with his son a ritual they did whenever they could. He explained that it felt good to be out in nature, teaching his son its value. Some parents had date nights with their children. The father would take his daughter out for a date night, or the mother would take her son out. This enabled the parent of the opposite sex to have some time with the children and teach them how to treat others.

Make some of your own fun traditions. Also, make sure to take lots of pictures and videos of these events. Your children will watch them and look at them for hours when they are older. It will remind them of how much they are loved. Saying "I love you" is imperative, but showing it is just as important.

The Value of Time with Extended Family

Your children's extended family can really add a lot to their lives and even make up for times when the nuclear family is torn apart. When children do not feel comfortable talking to their parents, they may feel like they can talk to an extended family member, like a grandparent. This may ensure some of the same values and beliefs you hold are being presented to your children.

One parent who went through a divorce said she and her children got closer to her extended family during that difficult time, and it really helped out. Even if you live far away from your extended family, you can still build the relationships through vacations, holidays, and phone calls. Another parent talked about the fact that even though her extended family lives all over the country, they keep in touch through phone calls, Facebook, and e-mail.

Grandparents, aunts, uncles, and cousins can play an important role in your children's lives. If you live far away from them, you can still have those relationships by creating special times together. Whether it is a summer vacation at the beach each year or sharing a special holiday together, these times can be an important part of your children's lives. In my family, we have been fortunate to make our extended family vacations an important ritual we do at least twice a year.

If you do not have an extended family, you can still build one for your child through close friends and neighbors. The community a child grows up in can be a powerful support network. Some of our great family traditions were made with my neighbors, because my extended family was far away. For many years, we had a neighborhood Fourth of July picnic and parade. All the children would decorate their bikes or other moving items and ride up and down the street. I can still picture their smiling faces as they rode. Halloween was also a neighborhood event where we all brought food to the cul-de-sac and ate dinner together before trick or treating began. A neighborhood can be a great substitute if your family is far away. You may have to the one who takes the initiative and starts these wonderful traditions in yours.

Teens I know maintain how important it is to know their neighbors. For many of them, their neighbors became like their families, and being part of a close neighborhood helped them grow up. They played games like kickball for hours in the street and learned to come together as a community. In those neighborhood games, they learned to be mediators and built friendships. They were not indoors playing video games; they were outside with each other, enjoying their neighborhood "family" members.

Leave a Lasting Memory

I didn't realize how important family time was to my children until my oldest daughter went away to college. We usually tried to have a family night one Friday night every couple of months when our children were little. We would either watch a favorite movie or play a game. However, as my older daughter became a teenager, this became tougher to do because she always wanted to be with her friends. We did have to make her do it on several occasions, and inevitably, she had fun. The ironic thing was the first weekend she came home from college her freshman year, she insisted on everyone staying home and having a family night. I was pleasantly shocked; we had to force my teenage son to stay, but he came around.

Be sure to keep traditions going each year. It builds great memories of family time. All these traditions help connect the family, and your children will grow to value them over the years, likely passing down some of these traditions to their own children. Even when your children are busy in sports or other activities, find a way to keep the traditions intact, even when family time becomes limited.

Don't let those teenage years stop the family time, even if your children complain. In the end, they cherish these times and will someday be the ones who instigate them, just as my daughter did on that first weekend home from college. Children learn the importance of family through their parents. The time you invest in them will come back to you later when they are older. They will be the ones talking about family time and how important it is, because you instilled this value in them.

Chapter 7 - Having Choices and Figuring Out Problems

"If you want children to keep their feet on the ground, put some responsibility on their shoulders."[xiv] (Abigail Van Buren)

When I was starting my family, I had no idea how many obstacles I would face as a mother, a wife, and a career woman. One of the biggest obstacles I have had to overcome in my life was learning not to worry so much. See, I come from a long line of worriers. My grandmother fretted all too often, and my father still worries about the family a lot today. In fact, I can even remember worrying about my parents' safety at a young age. A little worrying may be good, but when it consumes us and keeps us from living full, healthy lives or from allowing our children to lead their lives, it is a problem. My life was literally consumed with worry at one point. I knew I had a problem—the same problem many of you may be facing today as you consider how to keep your children safe and secure in a world that is often unsure and unstable.

Allison Merkle Alison

My worrying became almost obsessive after the birth of my first child. I can remember being home on maternity leave and holding my two-week-old daughter in my arms as I watched a show on television titled "Babysitters, Baby Killers." I know; what was I thinking, right? When it was over, I was upset and called my mother, telling her I could never find anyone to watch my daughter when I went back to practicing law. The first thing she told me was to stop watching shows like that, and then she assured me I would find someone I could trust. She was right too; I did find a wonderful nanny for my daughter who even helped raise my son when he was born.

For many years when my children were young, I imagined terrible things happening to them and constantly feared losing them. I was truly consumed with dread that something terrible would happen to them. It probably did not help that I worked in the child abuse and neglect court and saw a lot of misfortune. Even when my husband and I would finally hire a babysitter and get a night out together, I would worry the entire time, so I could not enjoy myself. At the time, I thought that if I controlled everything in my children's lives, I could keep them safe. I actually would have liked to put them in a bubble to always protect them. The only problem was that I was not letting my children grow up to be independent people and instead tried to control everything and everybody to protect my children from harm.

I realized I needed to find a better way of looking at life, because my years were passing me by while I was so consumed with worry. I also started thinking that I did not want to pass this worrying along to my children. I watched them with their free spirits and joy for life, and I did not want to kill that carefree happiness by teaching them to worry. I finally started reading books about the power of the mind, about letting go of worry, and about being present in the moment. I learned to tell myself that well-being is the normal state, and the catastrophes are not. I formed a new routine instead of worrying too. For example, when I started to worry about my children when they were not in my presence, I literally said "well-being, well-being, well-being" in my head to stop the crazy thoughts. It was my mantra to remind me that they were fine.

Throughout my years of parenting, I have had to learn a valuable lesson, one affirmed by the knowledgeable parents I interviewed when learning about how they had been successful as parents. The fact is that having too much control over our children is not healthy. When they are young, they need our guidance and they need us to teach them right from wrong. But as they get older, we must let them have some control over their lives or they will rebel. Or, even worse, if they feel like they have no control over their lives, it can lead to dangerous behaviors like cutting, eating disorders, and substance abuse. These behaviors can also occur when one totally neglect his or her child, as neglect is also a control issue but with the opposite effect. I have seen all these results as an attorney and teacher, and I have learned that parenting is a balancing act. You have to be present in their lives and teach them to be independent all at the same time.

Allowing and Teaching Choice as Children Grow and Mature

In the early years, parents must teach children right from wrong through their words and actions, but as children get older, parents must not keep telling them what do to. We must, instead, instill in them the desire to do what is right—a desire that needs be created when they are young. You do this by slowly teaching them how to make correct choices. As they learn to make the correct choices, they feel good about themselves. They want your approval, so when they see you are pleased by the choices they have made, they feel good about their decisions. Confidence comes from their successes, and there are many ways we can teach this confidence in making correct choices as they are maturing.

For example, when your children are young, give them choices, like choosing the clothes to wear each day. If you are worried they will go to school in shorts in the winter, you can pick out three outfits and let them choose from the three. As a side note, do it the night before so the morning is not stressful. You can also allow them to choose a snack, but limit the choices if you don't want them eating unhealthy. In these simple things, your children get to learn how to make choices, but the outcome is fine with you either way. By giving them reasonable alternatives and making them part of the decision making, you are creating a learned skill. In this way, when they have to make big decisions someday, they will be better able to.

When your children start school, help them do their homework by setting up a homework location that is free from distractions, being present to make sure they get the work done, and helping them if they don't understand their assignments. Don't do the work for them; this rule includes projects. Even if it might help them get a good grade, it does not help them in the long run. Instead, let go and observe. Watch your children do what they can do. The parents' role is to instill ideals and values in their children so they can do things on their own. As situations come up, such as the aforementioned projects, they will show you they can handle things; in return, your need to control them will come to rest, so you can watch them shine.

As children get older, around the late elementary school years and middle school years, you need to back off and let them do more on their own. Hopefully by this point, doing their schoolwork is a habit, like brushing their teeth. However, during this transition period, they may miss one or two homework assignments. This is your chance to teach them about making the correct choices. They need to learn the consequence of not doing it so that when they get to the teen years and high school-level work they don't make those mistakes.

It is important that children learn these lessons before entering high school, because grades in high school will have an impact on the possibility of attending college and what colleges they can attend. You need to help them develop the skill of good choices before that time. Let them see that missing those assignments hurts their grade point average before high school. Or let them find out that doing their big science project at the last minute may not earn a good grade. You need to be aware and present when all this is going on; you just shouldn't control it all for them. Talk to your children about the choices they made and even have consequences for not getting assignments done on time, but let them make the choices at some point. Hopefully, they will learn from them.

Also expose them to different activities to see what they are interested in, but always let them make the choices on what they like to do or do not enjoy. Don't force them to take part in an activity if they don't like doing it. You can tell them you want them to be involved in activities, but let them choose between several different things. If you are concerned they will choose something dangerous or an activity that is too expensive, limit their choices. Being involved in sports or other activities can help children develop social skills and keep them out of trouble too, which are great reasons to encourage them to get involved. Just don't over schedule them; remember that they need time each day to play.

When your children choose particular activities, you need to support them too. You need to attend games or recitals as much as you can. Many of us have seen children on teams or in social events where their parents never show up to support them. You can literally see the pain in the children's faces when there is no one there for them. Children just need to feel like they matter, and it shows you support their choices when you are there for them. You send the message that they matter by making family attendance a priority, no matter the age of the child. If you can't attend due to work, ask a grandparent or other family member to attend in your place.

Several "star students" I have known through my experiences as a teacher have discussed how being involved in sports helped them make friends and feel accomplished. They learned that being on a team can teach drive and competition, but, they caution, it is not for everyone. Don't force your children to be involved in sports if they are not interested. Let them find their passion. You don't want them to rebel because you are pushing your passion on them. The parent's passion may not be the same as the child's.

Another student talked about his passions for music. This was instilled in him in the third grade when his parents made him try the piano and learn to play it. It was a requirement in the family for all the children to learn to play the piano at that age. Music became very important to him and brought him discipline, he explained. When he got older, he chose to play the trumpet. He talked about the fact that playing the trumpet brought him such joy and became his true passion. He went on to say, "Music has a special quality about it. Languages divide cultures, but music is universal. Everyone can understand it. It takes away our differences."

You can also teach your children to be responsible by giving them chores and setting expectations. Tell them they need to clean their rooms by a certain time, and if it isn't done, then there will be a certain consequence. They are making the choice to do what you ask or deal with the consequence. Also, let them start making their own lunches or doing their own laundry as they get older. They may not do it exactly the way you like them to do it, but they are taking responsibility little by little so that they can function on their own. During summer vacation in high school, let them get summer jobs or do volunteer work to help them learn to function in other settings. These part-time jobs can bring valuable lessons and teach responsibility.

Another area where you can allow choices is in allowing them to have a say in the way their rooms are decorated. This is particularly important when they are teenagers. If you are concerned about what they may pick, give them several choices. In any choice you give them, narrow the options by giving them a group to pick from; that way, it does not matter what they pick. Many of us did not think to involve our children in decorating their rooms, and we wished we had because it is such a simple way to give them a voice in their lives.

Other big choices they will be making in their lives one day are deciding what college to go to or what career to pursue. One parent talked about the fact he had taught his daughter to make choices throughout her life, so he felt confident in allowing her to make the important decision about what college she would attend. Her actions up to that point had been reasonable, and she had a history of making good choices. Again, when children are making this big college decision, parents can still set parameters, like selecting an in-state school or picking a career that will pay the bills. This man's daughter had bought into this decision-making process from a young age, so when she was older, she was able to do it on her own and make sound choices about higher education.

By the way, watching your children go off to college hurts, and you will miss them, but it is also an exciting time in their lives. You would not want them to live in your basement for the rest of their lives.

"Being the Parent" and Limiting or Eliminating Choice

There are many areas, however, where parents have to make the choices and children do not get to decide, especially when children are young. For example, at dinnertime, there is one meal prepared, and that's what everyone eats. If you allow your children to choose their own dinners every night, not only will you stress out the cook, but you will also create picky eaters. They need to learn to sit down to a meal and try new things. In this instance, the choice they could be making is to eat the meal or not eat anything until morning or not get dessert.

Also, if children choose an activity or sport that they are not ready for yet, they may need to wait until they are older. One example would be contact football; this is not a choice. They need to go to bed at a certain time so they can be up and ready for school. When children are young, they need to sit in a car seat, and when they are older, they need to wear a seat belt. These are nonnegotiable restrictions—not decisions your children may opt in or out of—because you don't want to put them in danger.

Another point some parents are very adamant about is not allowing tattoos and piercings until their kids are out of college. Consider that even at these late ages, they still need you to be the parent and set limits, but by giving them growing choices as they mature, they learn valuable decision-making skills for when they are older.

Allowing Yourself to Gain Perspective and Lose Some Control

By teaching your children to make responsible choices throughout their lives, you are helping them learn so that when the teenage years come along you can trust them to do the right thing. At some point, you will have to let them out of your control and hope they will make good decisions. Your children also have to know you believe in them and trust them.

Your children also need to know there are consequences for their actions. They need to learn to figure out their own solutions to their problems without you always rushing in to fix things. You can help your children by talking to them and helping them figure out what to do.

When they are young, you will make decisions for them often because they are unable to do it on their own, but as they get older, you must teach them to make decisions on their own. They will earn the right to make important decisions. It is a skill they need to develop over time, so they can function without you when they are on their own. You can even allow family votes on certain issues as your children get older. For example, you can allow them to vote on where the family goes out to eat or takes a vacation. Not only does this teach them decision-making skills, but it also makes them feel part of the family.

You may not always like the decisions your children make, but at some time in their lives, they have to take ownership of their lives. Also, remember that they are always watching you and how you make decisions in your own life. Finally, pick your battles and leave the little things up to them.

One of the toughest times for parents is when their children start to drive. Allowing teens to drive on their own is a big leap of faith. Hopefully, you have engrained your values in your children and taught them to act responsibly, so they will be good, law-abiding drivers. You will be really glad you taught them to be independent and reliable when they get behind a wheel of a car by themselves.

Another hard-earned lesson for us parents is knowing when to let go. As your children get older and older, they are going to ask to do things where you won't be present to control the situations. These are opportunities to see if they can make good choices and be responsible. As they show you they can be responsible in one situation, they can move up to more challenging situations.

For example, when they ask you to do things like go to a movie with a friend, consider if it is a reasonable request. If they are eight or nine years old, this may be too young to allow them to go the movies alone. So in this instance, you can tell them you will take them to the movies, but you will sit somewhere else in the theater. Explain to them that they are not ready to totally go on their own yet. Also, explain that there will come a time when they will be able to go alone. If, however, they are twelve or thirteen years old and are going with a responsible friend to an early movie, this may be a good chance to test them and give them a feeling of independence. You have to do things in stages. That is how children learn responsibility. You don't want to throw them into a situation they are too young to handle. Know your children and give them responsibilities and allow them to be in situations you think they can handle.

One of the most difficult decisions for parents is when their middle school children ask to go to their first boy/girl party. Many parents will instantly say, "Not until you are in high school." Middle school is a tough time, and children are really starting to exert their independence. If they are in sixth or seventh grade, you might say, "Not this year but maybe in eighth grade when you are a little older." It really depends on your children's maturity and the situation at the party.

Whatever age you allow them to start attending parties or any other similar events, don't be afraid to call the parents holding the function. Even if your children claim they will be mortified if you call, call. In fact, it is important to call and find out what type of supervision will be taking place. Again, you don't want to put your children in situations they are not ready to handle. Also don't just allow them to go to something because they claim everyone else is going or tell you "Ann's mom lets her." We have all heard this, but when parents actually talk to each other, we usually realize each child is saying the same thing just using a different name.

In the end, don't allow your children to go to any function, any vacations, or any events unless you know all the details and feel comfortable. Don't be afraid to say no to your teenager if you don't feel comfortable about the situation. But remember that there is balance, and at some point, you will have to let them go. You don't want their first experience making decisions to be in college. Instead, teach them how to make decisions in stages so they can learn gradually.

Coaching Your Children through Adversity

Children have to learn to deal with adversity. There may come a time in your children's lives when you can no longer be there. When you die, you want your children to be happy, functioning adults. In order for that to occur, you have to teach them how to handle life's situations. You need to show them how to problem solve when issues arise, and you need to help them develop skills to figure out problems.

It can be very tough to watch your children go through a difficult time, but it is also an opportunity for them to learn. You can be there to listen and ask questions to help them figure things out. Sometimes your children just need to figure it out. It is in some of the toughest life challenges that great gifts are found.

When your children come to you upset, you can ask them if they want you to help them solve a problem or just need to vent. One parent talked about the fact that her family had to move a lot when her son was growing up. This was very difficult for him, because he had to continually make new friends. She was empathetic to his challenge and listened to him. She worried about putting him through these frequent moves, but later on, she realized it taught him to make friends easily. No matter where he went when he was older, he always made friends. This hardship in his youth was a gift.

Sometimes you may need to tell them, "Don't just sit around and cry; figure it out." Encourage them to get quiet and think about things. For example, if your son has a coach who he feels is being unfair to him, encourage him think about how he can handle the situation so he can still enjoy the sport. Teach your children to "turn it around." How can they make the situation better? This is a great question to teach your kids to consider when they face troubling situations.

One of the best things to teach your children is to remember that they can't change people, but they can change how they react to people. They can't change the coach, the teacher, or the friend who is being a jerk, but they can change how they react to that person. This is a powerful concept to learn, as it empowers your children to know they do have options and they are not totally powerless in the situation. There is a saying that states, "Things work out for those who make the best of the way things turnout." You and your children can make the best of anything too.

One parent recalled her son's inability to stay organized. She'd tried everything she could think of since he was young and finally asked him to think of ways to solve the problem. They tried calendars, agendas, and even spoke into a tape recorder. Then one day he just got it, and it was rarely an issue after that. As illustrated by this example, helping your children think of ways to solve their problems themselves teaches them how to solving problems, but solving the problem for them only fixes the problem.

Stay Calm and Keep It in Perspective

Parents who hover over their children constantly and don't let them make decisions are often referred to as helicopter parents. You need to be an active parent, but there needs to be balance. If you do everything for your children, you cripple them. One parent talked about the fact that her mother did everything for her, and she was determined to make sure her own children were more independent. We, as parents, teach this by letting our children take responsibility for themselves. If you do everything for them and are making all their decisions, you take away their ability to learn how to be independent. Be nurturing but remember to teach them independence.

I heard a great statement once; "Worrying is focusing on the things you don't want to have in your life." It did not make sense to constantly focus on the things I did not want to happen when I was so gripped with worry in the past, especially when I also learned about the law of attraction. The law of attraction simply means that what you focus your attention on will come to you whether it is positive or negative. So instead of worrying and imagining the worst, I now focus on what I would like see happen in my life and my children's lives. I picture my children happy, healthy, and enjoying life, and you know what? That is exactly how their lives are going.

I know that bad things can happen at any time and to anyone, but I am choosing to enjoy life and be present in the moments with my family and friends instead of worrying about the what ifs. It would be very sad if I spent my children's entire childhoods worrying about every little thing they did or wanted to do instead of being present enjoying the time I had with them. I can't put them in a bubble or control everything to keep them safe, but I can be present today and enjoy what I have, knowing and hoping that whatever challenges come my way in life, I can handle them. I also put faith in the fact that my kids will be ready to face life's challenges too, because I have taught them how to face adversity and make decisions for themselves.

Oh, and by the way, I have learned not to watch movies or television or read books about bad things happening to children. I don't watch the news unless it is about an event I choose to learn more about. My imagination already runs rampant; I don't need to fuel the flames. If you are a worrier, like my natural inclination, stop subjecting yourself to these negative images and stories. It is not healthy for you or your children.

Allison Merkle Alison

Nothing is better in life than seeing your young children grow up into responsible, good citizens. Watching them go off and lead happy lives on their own, independent of you—well, I guess they are never totally independent, but mostly independent—is what parenting is all about. It is hard to see your child hurting, but remember that there are lessons to be learned through life experiences. You want your children to grow up and be good, law-abiding citizens. In order to do this, they have to learn about making the correct choices. In short, you need to prepare them to be independent.

Chapter 8 - Mistakes and Forgiveness

"The family is both the fundamental unit of society as well as the root of culture. It … is a perpetual source of encouragement, advocacy, assurance, and emotional refueling that empowers a child to venture with confidence into the greater world and to become all that he can be."[xv] (Marianne E. Neifert)

As parents, we often joke that we wish our kids came with an instruction manual. If they did, it might read a little something like this:

Note to Parent:

We will make mistakes. We have to make our own mistakes so we can learn. You can't protect us from this by telling us about your mistakes and hoping we will not make mistakes because you did; instead, we have to learn on our own through our life experiences.

When we do something you are not proud of, remember why you had us to begin with. Remember the feeling of joy and the fact you would have given anything to have us during those days when you were expecting and anticipating our arrival. Remember that we are your children. You brought us into the world for happiness and love. Defend us always.

We are not perfect. We need to know that it is okay to have problems and mess up. It can be so hard on us to try and be perfect all the time for you. We like all the praise and awards, but then it can be scary if we make a mistake. We feel anxious and stressed trying to always be perfect. When we are trying to be perfect and looking for self-validation and praise from others all the time, we don't learn how to love ourselves. As a result, all the awards and praise will never be enough, so we are never truly happy.

Please be there for us when we do mess up. Above all else, teach us to love ourselves, faults and all.

When life gives your children tough lessons, teach your children how to deal with them. Make the best of adversity and teach your children that they can get through anything because learning to deal with adversity and challenges is crucial in life. Teach them to pick themselves up and do better next time; they need to understand that it is not the end of the world. Instill in them the belief that together you can fix problems, discussing possible solutions with them so that the same problems aren't likely to happen again.

Even if it feels overwhelming when you are involved in the troubles of your children and you are just so tired of it all, you must be there for your children and teach them to do better. Just remember, "This too shall pass."

Teaching Children How to Deal with Adversity

I remember an incident with my son when he was about seven years old. Like a lot of little boys, my son was an energetic and athletic little guy who seemed to always be in motion except when he was sleeping. Usually, this did not present a problem, but one day I was alerted to a problem that stemmed from this rambunctious nature of his.

A neighbor came to me upset because my son had knocked into his daughter pretty hard on the trampoline and did not even seem to care. I talked to my son, and he immediately stated, "I didn't mean to hurt her. I was just jumping around." I knew he had not intentionally hurt her, but he needed to learn that even though he had not intentionally meant to hurt someone, he had and he needed to apologize.

I had him write a little apology note (which was another good lesson in writing) to bring to her. The note only said something like, "I am sorry I hurt you. I did not mean to." It was written by him in his little, barely readable, second-grade handwriting. I walked down to her house with him, but I let him walk up to the door to deliver it. He came back with a smile on his face and seemed to feel better about the situation. Gone was the shame he felt for hurting someone.

It was funny that I felt so much pride seeing him deliver that letter. Although this was such a little incident and certainly not something to make into a big deal, I did need to teach him to apologize even if he had unintentionally hurt someone. It was a little incident with a big lesson.

Like my son and my daughters, your children are going to make mistakes; every child does. Even the children you think are perfect have made mistakes. No one is perfect. Teenagers, in particular, think they are invincible and do stupid things. Your children need to know that you will always be there for them no matter what. This is unconditional love. Allow them to experience the consequences from their mistakes but know you support them; remember that these same mistakes are opportunities to learn and will help them with their self-confidence. These are the teachable moments in life.

When your children face problems and make mistakes, remember that they are not bad people, but for whatever reason, they made bad decisions that led to these mistakes. You may even have to point out to your children that they are good people who made some bad decisions. You must be flexible and know it will all work out. Let your children live their lives and know they will make mistakes, but also know they will be taught valuable life lessons from these experiences. Give them space to make mistakes; however, don't let your children get into situations that will put them in danger or cause them to make decisions where the consequences are enormous.

Learning to apologize (the lesson I taught my son when he was seven) is an important lesson and shows respect for others. Teaching children to say, "I am sorry" when they hurt someone teaches them empathy too. Teaching them to apologize when they are wrong will help them learn to take responsibility and move on. They do not have to hold on to the mistakes, but they do need to make amends. When they learn to say "I am sorry" and mean it, they also learn about forgiveness, which is important for their souls. Other people will make mistakes that may affect them, and they need to learn to let those go too.

If your children make mistakes, they may have to earn back your trust before you allow them to be in certain situations again. Explain to them that you will get through this; they can earn back your trust, but it may take a little time. You want them to not want to disappoint you again. Talk about what they learned from the incident and make sure they got the lesson, but be careful to not belabor the issue so long that they stop caring. They have to know you will attempt to trust them again at some point, so they can prove they can do better and show what they learned from it all.

For example, when teenagers first learn to drive, especially boys, they think the car is a toy and often exhibit risky behavior. I can't tell you the number of times students have come to me for advice about a speeding or reckless driving ticket because they know I am an attorney. This is a good opportunity to talk and learn about the risks of speeding and the responsibly of driving. If they don't learn from this lesson, there will be a bigger one down the road. Usually the lessons get more serious and come with bigger consequences, so explain to your children that a ticket might actually be a gift, of sorts, and that next time they might not be so lucky.

If your children wreck the car, they can learn from the experience by having to pay for the damages. Also, they can learn from the accident and slow down. The little accidents can help teach a valuable lesson so there are not big accidents. These little things could actually be blessings in disguise, so don't overreact and think that the world has ended. Instead, let your children learn and allow them to deal with the consequences of their mistakes, but let them know you are there to back them up. This teaches them responsibility.

When difficult times occur, the extended family can help. It is important for children to have other adults they can talk to and that you can turn to for support, help, or advice. If your children stop listening to you, another member of the family may be able to get through to them when they need help. For example, one parent remembered when her son really had a bad attitude and was driving her crazy. It helped when her father-in-law came and picked up her son and spent time with him. He had a little talk with him, and her son came back with an adjusted attitude.

Another way we can help our children learn to deal with adversity is by not holding grudges because of their mistakes. Be sure to let each day be a clean slate, because each day they should get a chance to do better. This reminds them that even though they mess up, you still expect them to pick themselves up and move on.

If you continue to hold their mistakes over their heads, they will feel defeated and may shut down to the point that they stop trying to do well. Instead, give them the chance to redeem themselves and don't keep throwing past mistakes in their faces. Also, remember that you will make mistakes too, and your children will be watching how you handle them because you are their most important teacher in life. As a parent, you will make mistakes, and you will lose it from time to time. You will also overreact and feel regret, but you can teach your children the power of apologies and forgiveness through your actions.

Learning from the Veteran Pros

While interviewing highly successful parents, they spoke at length about the mistakes their kids had made and the problems their kids had faced along the way. Their stories are ones that resonate with many parents, ones that help us understand the importance of teaching our kids how to deal with adversity.

For example, one parent relayed the story about her daughter who had an incident when she had lied to her teacher. The mother had told her children previously that if there was an issue at school and if the teacher might call home, she wanted to hear from them first and not be surprised by the teacher. Her daughter did tell her about the incident, though, so they talked about how she could and should have handled it. Her daughter, with her help, decided it was best to go talk to the teacher and apologize. Her mother went with her for two reasons: one, to show support of her and, two, to make sure the teacher was not rude to her. If the teacher had been rude, she would have stepped in. In the end, it all worked out, and her daughter learned a valuable lesson about lying. This example shows us to support our children but also make sure they do the right thing, taking advantage of opportunities to learn and mature.

One parent talked about the time her ninth grade daughter had an unsupervised party at their house where alcohol was served without her knowledge. She had always encouraged her children to have friends over and wanted her home to be the house where teenagers felt comfortable hanging out; however, feeling comfortable to this extent was not what she intended. She and her husband came home to find the party, and they proceeded to pour out the beer and call all the parents of the children who were at the party to let them know what had happened. This was, of course, mortifying to the girl, but the parents believed it was necessary since the party had taken place in their home. The woman then spoke to her daughter about the dangers of underage drinking and explained that she was not old enough to drink alcohol. She used this mistake to teach her about the dangers of alcohol and the danger in putting the family at risk by having the party.

Another parent recalled an incident with her son in high school when he made a statement on the computer about someone in the community, which landed him in criminal court. This was difficult on the family and at the time felt overwhelming; they even had to hire an attorney to work things out. It was tough because they lived in a community where everyone knew each other. A deal was eventually reached, and there were consequences for his actions but none so severe that it kept him from becoming the successful man he is today. At the time, however, it seemed devastating

The parent went on to say that looking back at the situation so many years later reminded her that you can get through anything. You can't give up on your children because they make mistakes; instead, make lessons out of these mistakes. It is hard to think this way when you are totally immersed in the situation and feel so overwhelmed, but remember that you can get through it and you will. Believe it or not, most of these mistakes will be situations that you will look back on someday and laugh about.

One mother I interviewed spoke at length about the years of dealing with her son's substance abuse and depression. Her son had grown up a happy, well-adjusted child until the middle school years when he started self-medicating because he could not sleep at night. She did not realize this was going on and all the other issues that she would later learn about until the drugs already had a hold on him.

The ironic thing is that her oldest child was the homecoming queen, the star athlete, the brain with the high GPA—in short, the child who had it all—so dealing with her troubled son was a new experience for her. She was not someone who gave up, though, so she made sure to get her son all the help she could. She realized early on the problem was not something she could deal with on her own, so she researched all her options and found the best help she could afford. Someone once asked her how she would pay for his college if she used all the money on his recovery, and she responded, "If I don't do everything now, college won't be an option." She knew she only had a few years before he would be an adult and making his own choices. At that point, she would have no control over the situation.

In the end, he received extensive counseling, attended a wilderness camp, and ended up going to a private school where he got more one-on-one help. She never gave up on him, and he did eventually attend college. This story demonstrates an important point: if your children have substance abuse issues or suffer from a major illness like depression, you must do everything you can to get them help. You cannot solve these problems on your own; instead, you must get professional help and try to find a support network of parents who are going through the same thing. It will help you realize you are not alone and can get through it.

Another parent talked about her grown daughter who made a mistake and how it was extremely difficult on the family. The ironic thing was that what they thought was one of the worst things that could happen to them actually brought them closer as a family. Their daughter, who was legally old enough to drink alcohol, made the critical mistake of getting in her car after drinking one night and got pulled over for a DUI. She was taken into custody, strip searched, made to wear a jail uniform, and put behind bars. Talk about having to deal with the consequences!

After she was released, they had to get an expensive attorney, go through the court system, and complete the court-ordered programs as part of the plea deal for this crime. It was an extremely painful and trying time for the entire family. The young woman was ashamed and humiliated for what she had done, but she clearly learned a valuable lesson. What this parent and her daughter realized was that being pulled over was really a blessing, because it could have been worse. She could have killed herself or someone else.

Another thing this parent learned was that she had played a part in this mistake, because she had not really talked with her daughter about the consequences of drinking and driving. In fact, she herself had sometimes enjoyed a few drinks at restaurants throughout her life in front of her daughter and had driven a car home. She felt she had sent the wrong message and could have done better teaching her about the possible consequences of drinking and driving.

Finally, one of the biggest lessons from the entire painful experience was that as a family they could get through anything together. Don't wait until your children make this mistake to talk to them about the dangers of drinking and driving. Have the discussion and also let them know that you will always come get them if they have been drinking or will pay for their taxi if needed.

Allison Merkle Alison

Closing Thoughts

I can't state enough the importance of teaching your children that no problem is so big that they can't handle it. The teen suicide rate is too high, and according to the National Institute for Mental Health, suicide is the third leading cause of death among teens in the United States.[xvi] There are many reasons children may take their lives, but if they learn they can overcome anything and that you are there for them, the likelihood of it happening is far less.

One story that I will always recall that helped me realize just how important this is involves a young man in my community. I tell you this story not to scare you, but so you can learn from this tragedy. I have nothing but respect and empathy for the family involved and hope that by sharing this story it will not happen again. A couple years ago, this young man was driving his car with his friends as passengers. He got into an accident, and one of his friends was severely injured and taken to the hospital. The young man went home believing he had seriously injured his friend. While his parents went to the hospital to see how the injured young man was doing, he hanged himself at home. We will never know what was going on in his head or why he did it, but all of us in the community felt immense empathy and pain for the family. Many of us sat our own children down and told them the story in order to teach them that there is nothing they could do that we could not help them figure out a solution to and that suicide should never be the solution.

Another story that personally taught me that there is no problem or mistake that cannot be overcome involved every parent's worst nightmare. One of my close friend's nephew was going through a difficult time after losing his father to cancer his senior year in high school. He made an unimaginable mistake by driving with alcohol in his system and killed two people. He almost died himself. He not only had a long battle recovering physically but also had to deal with the fact he had killed two people. He went through the court system and spent two years in jail for what he had done and is now on a very long, restrictive probation.

I remember when I first heard about this case. I was so distraught. Here was a normal high school senior boy, and his life changed instantly with one terrible decision. I was so upset that I sat my children down again and discussed the dangers of drinking and driving. This was one of my worst nightmares.

At the time, I truly believed this young man's life was over. I mean, how could he recover from this and go on? But three years later, I found myself sitting in an auditorium listening to this young man speak to other high school students after being released from jail. I was honestly shocked and so happy to see that this young man had walked through all the pain, did his time, and was able to relay his powerful message to these kids. No adult, video, or gruesome tale could convey what he was saying to them.

When the question part came in the presentation, I asked him, "How did you get through all of this?" He replied very passionately, "With the help of my family." I realized then and there that there is no problem you can't get through. If he could make it through that and be okay, then we can all get through our trials. The key is the love and support of family, and with that, you can get through anything.

Even though that is an extreme example, I wish there were a place before criminal court that young people could be sent to handle some of the mistakes they make. Often what should be a teachable moment can become a criminal record. Zero tolerance in schools never made sense to me, because school should be the place where you learn lessons. We don't just teach facts and dates; we teach social skills. Hopefully, when our children graduate, they will become good law-abiding citizens. Even top students make stupid mistakes that can affect them.

It always amazes me as a teacher to see young people who are so phenomenal not feel good enough. They do stupid things, like cheat on tests because they are afraid of not getting an A. They certainly are capable of working hard to get the A, but somewhere along the way they decided cheating would be better or easier or, perhaps, they put so much pressure on themselves to achieve that they resorted to cheating. I see these times as teachable moments when I can try and relay the importance of good character over grades. I don't judge students solely on one incident. I see it as a time in their lives when they are asserting their independence but still figuring out what it entails.

    Life usually gives us little bumps in the road from which to learn, especially when we are continually displaying risky behavior. When we don't listen to the little bumps or lessons, then we get bigger ones. Teach your children to listen and learn from the little bumps, so they won't have to endure the big ones. Teach yourself to accept the fact that your kids are not perfect and never will be, either, granting forgiveness liberally, just as you would want if the situation were reversed.

Chapter 9 - Role Model

"Don't worry that children never listen to you; worry that they are always watching you."[xvii] *(Robert Fulghum)*

How many times have we heard the old parenting adage "Do as I say, not as I do"? Don't we wish it were that easy?

"Do as I say, not as I do" does not work. Remember, you are the role models in your children's lives.

Consider that your children are always watching you, and children learn a great deal by watching their parents. Children copy what they see. You must parent them and be a role model to them, not trying to be their friend, especially in the teenage years. They have enough friends. When they are grown adults, then you can have a friendship. In fact, it will just naturally evolve if you have a good relationship with them when they are young.

They are sponges, soaking in everything you do and say. When they are born, you receive these babies who are practically clean slates, and then you write on them; what kind of message will your behavior—not just your words—leave?

Allison Merkle Alison

Modeling a Positive Attitude and Healthy Habits

Since children learn more from our actions than our words, anytime we are around children, we can make an impression, so we must be careful. For example, when you are in the car and someone cuts you off, is that a reason to go crazy? Do you really want your children to see you flipping someone off and screaming obscenities? Remember that they are watching and learning from you.

Consider that if you want your children to have certain values, you must live your life with those values on display. For example, if you want them to be polite to others by saying "please" or "thank you," you must do the same. If you want them to respect you, you must respect them and others. If you want them to act responsibly, you must be responsible. If they see you as a respectable, responsible adult, they won't want to disappoint you.

Another way you can model a positive attitude is to enjoy your job so they will strive for the same in their own lives. One parent talked about the fact that her husband had worked at a very difficult job for ten years and did not like it. One day, he decided he could not do it anymore, even if the money was really good. They sat their daughters down and explained that he would be taking a new job that would pay a lot less, so they would have to adjust their spending. The good thing was that he would be able to spend more time with the family. The girls did not care about the money, and it all worked out, especially because her husband was much happier.

You can be a role model through other tough times in your life as well. Your children are watching how you handle the challenges life throws you. One parent talked about the fact his son learned a lot about determination through his mother, who was losing her sight. She is legally blind today and needs to rely on people for many everyday needs. Although it was very difficult to give up some of her independence, she did it with dignity and determination. Her son watched her go through this ordeal and still watches her find joy in life today. By overcoming this challenging, undesirable obstacle, she became his greatest teacher.

One parent, who was also a grandparent, had an epiphany with her granddaughter. When she visited her granddaughter, she noticed that whenever the girl's mother gave her a piece of fruit, she would waste half of it. She would eat half and throw the rest away. This seemed wasteful, but her mom let her do this.

So, when her granddaughter came to visit at the grandmother's house by herself and her granddaughter asked her for a banana, she only gave her half of the banana. Her granddaughter noticed this and asked her why she could not have the entire banana. She told her granddaughter she could have as much as she wanted but that she would give it to her in sections.

Her granddaughter asked why, and the woman explained that she had seen how the granddaughter wasted the fruit in her own house and did not want her to waste food in her house. Her granddaughter immediately replied, "I like how you do it." She went on to say, "When I grow up, I'll do it like you."

The grandmother was so taken aback by her granddaughter's statement. She did not have to nag her or complain about the way her daughter-in-law allowed her to waste food in their home. The grandmother did not make a big deal about it; she was just a role model for her granddaughter. Her granddaughter was watching her and decided to follow her example. This story reminds us that our actions and the way we carry ourselves can have influence.

Another parent talked about the fact that his father was not always truthful with him. It really bothered him growing up, so when he became a father, he taught his daughter the importance of being truthful through his words and his actions, striving to be a better role model.

Also consider that if you want religion to be a part of your children's lives, it's important to be the example. Having faith and making religion important in your life is the best way to teach your children about it. Let them see you happy in your spiritual life, and they too will want to pursue it.

One parent who was an English teacher was careful how she spoke and also corrected her children from a young age, urging them to use proper grammar and speak in correct English. These corrections will help your children in life by teaching them to speak properly, making them more prepared for school and the workforce.

Speaking of language, if you expect good, clean language at home, you must use it yourself. If you don't want your children to use cuss words, then you have to watch what you say. You can tell kids there are bad words and that they should not use them, but then by using them yourself, you show differently. They will learn the language from you and repeat it. Whatever you say, they will say.

Consider too that you can talk to your children about having a good work ethic, but by having one yourself, you teach them so much more. In order to help them be successful, you need to show them what motivation and diligence are through your actions. You can be the smartest person, but if you are laziest, you won't be successful. You are modeling the behavior.

One parent talked about how his wife really taught their children about the value of hard work and education, because as their kids were growing up, she went from being a nurse to a doctor. They saw how hard she worked and witnessed her determination to succeed. Seeing you follow your dreams and be successful will give your children a great example to follow as well.

Sending the Right Messages about Substance Use and Abuse

Your children are watching you, and don't be surprised if they also acquire your addictions while watching. For example, if you drink alcohol in front of your children, don't be shocked when they do the same. In fact, children of alcoholics have a higher chance of becoming alcoholics when they are older. According to the Academy of Child and Adolescent Psychiatry, "Children of alcoholics are four times more likely than other children to become alcoholics."[xviii]

Of course, there are many children who grew up around alcoholic parents who made a conscious choice not to make the same mistake, but they had to be aware of the potential cycle of addiction and take steps to break it. For many parents who were children of alcoholic parents, they went out of their way to discuss this problem with their own children and the potentially higher risk for them. One parent totally stopped drinking when his son was born so that his son would not grow up and drink. Another parent stopped drinking around his children, because he did not want to embarrass them. He had grown up with an alcoholic mother who was abusive, and he did not want to put his children through that same situation.

Through my career, I have seen many children use drugs, and not surprising, so did their parents. If they see you using even what you think are harmless drugs, they will think nothing of trying it themselves.

If you smoke, chances are greater that your children will smoke; statistics show that if you smoke, your children are twice as likely to smoke.[xix] You may think you are only harming yourself with your addictions, but you are also harming your children through influence. You are setting the example for them and introducing them to these harmful habits.

My husband made a deal with his parents when he was young where he would receive a thousand dollars when he turned twenty-one if he did not ever try drugs or cigarettes. They did not make alcohol part of the deal. He said it helped him think twice about using and gave him an out with his friends. It also clearly let him know where his parents stood on the issue. Later, we tried it in our family too. I don't know how effective it was, because I am still in the throes of parenting my youngest daughter, but I do like the fact that it gives them an out.

When dealing with the tough topic of alcohol, drugs, tobacco, and potential addictions, have the conversations and be the role model. If you do drink alcohol around your children, teach them responsible drinking and avoid overindulging.

Modeling Emotional Strength and Anger Control

Not only are your children watching you and your habits, but by living with you, they learn to match your moods. We are products of the environment in which we grow up. If you are a moody and sad person, don't be surprised that your children will end up that way too.

Try not to allow your own negative moods to taint your children. Instead, your house should be a place children want to come home to and not one where they feel like they are constantly walking on eggshells and worrying that you might blow up or go off the deep end. Just try to do a little better and be the best you can be for your children. Be your authentic self and show them how to be happy, productive members of society.

If you had a stressful day at work, take ten or fifteen minutes to calm down and relax so you don't bring that stress and negativity to your home. Try to be a positive person and watch your temper.

Parenting at Our Best

One student I came to know in my experience as a teacher is one who was influenced in a negative manner by her father. She had a big impact on me; she reminded me to find the "joy" in life every day.

She was the first generation in her family to go to school in the United States, and she faced many cultural issues growing up here. At one point in her high school years, she became very lonely, sad, and even suicidal. When she finally stepped back and looked at what was causing some of these negative moods, she realized she was mirroring some of her father's patterns.

See, as she was growing up, she heard her father repeat negative statements, such as "You can't trust people," and she watched how he isolated himself and treated others poorly, particularly her mother. She had empathy for her father, because she believed a lot of his behavior might have been caused by the way people treated him because of his culture. However, it was difficult to be in the home and watch this behavior, and it took its toll on her.

She too was isolating herself at school and feeling like she could not trust people, but somewhere inside she knew she did not want to feel this way anymore. She finally got help and addressed these issues. She came to see how her father's negative behavior was making her feel the same way he did, and she did not like it. She started making a conscious effort to put herself out there and make friends. She also worked hard on changing her negative views to thinking more positive. She had to break the cycle before she ended up like him. It is still a battle for her today, but she knows now that she can have the life she wants by not mirroring her father's behavior.

Another child I represented as an attorney also demonstrated the power of parents as role models. I was appointed by the court to be the guardian ad litem to a teenage girl who was being criminally charged by her parents for destroying some of her mother's clothing and, more specifically, taking out her anger at her mom by using scissors to cut up some of her mother's clothing. There had been many issues in this family for years, and finally, the parents had had enough and had their own daughter arrested.

When I asked her why she had done it, she said she just lost it. She went on to say that her dad was a hypocrite, because she could recall many times when he lost it throughout her childhood. She remembered one night at the dinner table when she was about six years old and her dad got angry—so angry that he picked up the ketchup bottle and threw it against the wall. She remembered how the ketchup went everywhere and how scared she was watching it. This was just one of many incidents when her father lost it when he was angry. She was really indignant about the fact that her dad had her arrested for losing it, because she had learned this behavior from him. She wondered why no one ever called the police on him. It reminded me that our children are always watching us and learning behavior from us.

If you have anger issues and blow up a lot, you need to seek help to get it under control so you don't pass it on to your children. It is not okay to take your anger out on people, particularly the ones you say you love. Let me say this again: *it is not okay to take your anger out on people!*

Throughout my careers as an attorney and a teacher, I have witnessed the devastating effects this type of behavior has on children. From whom did most learn this behavior? Chances are it was one of their parents, because they are our biggest role models. We need to stop the cycle and do better for our children. There are so many resources available to people now to help; one can get help from professionals through counseling or group therapy and learn techniques like mediation, exercise, yoga, and deep breathing to control outbursts. There are a plethora of books on how to control anger and live a more peaceful life. You can do it. Do it for yourself and do it for your children. Don't let the cycle continue.

Breaking the Cycle of Anger and Ending Bullying

Another reason to learn to control your anger is that you may be creating a child who becomes a bully to others. When you take out your anger on your children and they learn that behavior, they may go to school and take it out on others. Your children may lash out at others, not knowing the damage they are causing. It is as if you are passing this anger from person to person.

I had a student who admitted to me and the class I was teaching that he had been a bully. I will never forget the day he shared that with us, as it was one of the most educational days in my life.

I had brought an article in to my government class about a bullying incident that had resulted in a teen suicide. The teenagers who had done the bullying were being criminally prosecuted for their actions. I had brought the article thinking we would have a discussion about whether these teens should be criminally prosecuted, but it turned into a discussion I will never forget.

After the students read the article, we started a discussion about it. One student said, "I know bullying is bad, but kids shouldn't commit suicide over it." After he made that statement, a student immediately spoke up and said, "You don't know how it feels to be bullied every day." We were all taken aback when we realized the student who spoke those words was one of the most popular and funny students in the school.

He had his head down, which was unusual for this tall, confident young man, and he went on to tell us about how he had been bullied all through middle school before he had come to our high school. He even admitted that suicide had crossed his mind. We were all in shock, and the emotion in the room was so raw that tears came to my eyes.

The next thing I knew, another student spoke about a time when she had stood by and watched another student being bullied and did nothing. She felt awful, even many years later. She said it was hard living with herself because she not stepped in and done something when she witnessed the bullying.

What got our attention next was the popular football star who admitted to being a bully and felt terrible about it. He said he bullied because his parents bullied him at home. He said the way he had grown up had taught him that behavior.

This was a senior class, so by this time in school, most of them felt confident in who they were and were able to share their feelings openly. While looking at all these amazing young people, I realized that we create the environments that can bring about good or bad in people. This was a powerful moment of realization for me.

One of the incredible things that came out of this class discussion is a tradition in our school now where the upper classmen hold an assembly for the younger students on antibullying. The students themselves actually speak and relay the message of not bullying and lending a hand to others.

What I have learned through this experience is that there will always be bullying, especially if parents continue to pass on their anger and do not help their children become good, caring people. But bullying in school is a teachable moment. We can unlearn this behavior and do better. By creating positive environments in a school where the students take ownership of an antibullying atmosphere, bullying can be decreased.

You don't have to parent the way your parents did if you did not like their style, but you must make the conscious effort to break the destructive cycles you may have inherited from them. Many of our little habits are engrained in us from our childhood. How often have you caught yourself sounding like one of your parents and been shocked by your behavior? You must break the cycle and be the person you want your children to grow up to be.

Also, if you make a mistake—and you will make many—admit when you are wrong and apologize. Show your children how this is done with dignity and grace. Being able to apologize when you are wrong is a sign of respect. Don't be afraid to say, "I'm sorry that I lost it. That was not okay." Also, by teaching them to apologize, they learn how to forgive. Both your children and you will make mistakes, but these times are opportunities to learn forgiveness.

The good thing is not only can you be a role model for inappropriate behavior, but you also can be one for good behavior. Live your life the way you would like to see your children live theirs. We are all different, and hopefully, they will go on to find their authentic selves, but they will still have grown up with you and picked up a lot of your traits. Make those traits ones you would be proud for them to exhibit. If you want them to eat healthy and exercise, the best thing you can do is eat healthy and exercise. If you want them to be respectful, good citizens, then you must exemplify good citizenship in your life. Be the person you want to see in your child. You are their greatest teacher. As the saying goes, actions speak louder than words.

Chapter 10 - Good Character, Respect, and Building Self-Esteem

"Self-esteem is the real magic wand that can form a child's future. A child's self-esteem affects every area of her existence, from friends she chooses, to how well she does academically in school, to what kind of job she gets, to even the person she chooses to marry."[xx] (Stephanie Martson)

We hear much about the beautiful and the wealthy, the famous and the glamorous. How much do we hear about those with good character, though?

Interestingly, a man we associate with wealth and fame, financier J.P. Morgan, said this of good character: "A man's best collateral is his character." As such, make sure to make a sound investment in your own child by instilling this good character through your teachings, your words, your actions, and the respect you hold for others.

Allison Merkle Alison

Teaching, Instilling, and Modeling Good Character

To put it bluntly, teach your children to be good people. Instill in them the values you want to see in them when they are older. Teach them to value work and dedication. Also teach them to value all people. Encourage them to be open-minded to all races and religions. Show them that each person has something to offer and that they can learn something from everyone. Encourage them to accept people for who they are and not judge them. Raise children who are respectful and whom you would want to be around when they are older. There are lots of beautiful and bright children, but you need to make sure you raise them to be good people.

The Josephson Institute Center for Youth Ethics defines good character as the following:

Trustworthiness

- Be honest.
- Don't deceive, cheat, or steal.
- Be reliable—do what you say you'll do.
- Have the courage to do the right thing.
- Build a good reputation.
- Be loyal—stand by your family, friends, and country.

Respect

- Treat others with respect; follow the Golden Rule.
- Be tolerant and accepting of differences.
- Use good manners, not bad language.
- Be considerate of others' feelings.

- Don't threaten, hit, or hurt anyone.
- Deal peacefully with anger, insults, and disagreements.

Responsibility

- Do what you are supposed to do.
- Plan ahead.
- Persevere—keep on trying!
- Always do your best.
- Use self-control.
- Be self-disciplined.
- Think before you act—consider the consequences.
- Be accountable for your words, actions, and attitudes.
- Set a good example for others.

Fairness

- Play by the rules.
- Take turns and share.
- Be open-minded; listen to others.
- Don't take advantage of others.
- Don't blame others carelessly.
- Treat all people fairly.

Caring

- Be kind.
- Be compassionate and show you care.

- Express gratitude.
- Forgive others.
- Help people in need.

Citizenship

- Do your share to make your school and community better.
- Cooperate.
- Get involved in community affairs.
- Stay informed; vote.
- Be a good neighbor.
- Obey laws and rules.
- Respect authority.
- Protect the environment.
- Volunteer. [xxi]

These are the six pillars taught at my school and many other schools across the country. It is not only up to the schools to teach these principles, but it is imperative that parents teach them as well. Imagine a world where all people lived by these principles. You can do your part to make the world a better place just by teaching your children to value these ideals. Religion and spirituality may also be good ways to teach the values you want to instill. Do the best you can to teach these lofty values.

For example, show your children how to be polite and courteous. You are the one to teach them good manners. Even when they are young, you can teach them. One parent always insisted that her children use good manners when they were eating, even if they were just at McDonald's. She always had them put their napkins on their laps. You can teach your children how to eat properly at a restaurant too. Show them how to politely ask for things in social situations. If you want them to have good manners when they are adults, you must instill good manners in them as they are growing up. Again, you show them all this not only through your words but your actions.

One student talked about the fact that she learned good manners at the day care center she attended growing up. She not only learned to act properly, but she also made many good friends she is still close to today. Being involved in this positive social setting really helped her grow into the independent, good person she is today.

Another important standard you must teach your children is to be honest and truthful. Truthfulness is very important. One parent used a difficult high school experience his son was going through to teach him integrity. The teen had played football all through high school and had been very dedicated to the team. He assumed his senior year that he would have the starting position he had played all the previous years. However, a new student moved into the area and got the position. He was very disappointed, and he sought advice from his father, who told him to work it out respectfully with his coach. The father did not step in but allowed his son to work it out.

In the end, the young man did not get the starting position he expected and desired, but because of his dedication and the fact he worked it all out with integrity, he did become one of the captains on the team. The coach saw him as a role model for the other players. This leadership role meant a great deal to the teen, and the respect he earned boosted his confidence greatly.

Since social occasions allow for growth, enroll your children in sports or other activities to help them to learn how to develop socially. Through sports, Cub Scouts, and other such activities, children can learn good character and how to get along with others. Make sure your children get involved in some of these activities to help build their self-confidence and teach them how to make friends.

Research shows that children who are able to get along well with others and who have friends in school are less likely to be bullied or become depressed. One parent talked about her son who was small and was often bullied. He struggled socially in high school, but in college, he became involved in what he liked to do and had many successes that built his confidence. Today he is a successful young man who one would never guess was bullied. This story illustrates an important point: don't cut your children off from others because you are afraid they will get hurt or be treated badly. These are the opportunities where children learn to be a good, social, cooperative people. When they get involved in outside activities, they evolve as people.

You can teach good character through your actions and words, but you can also teach bad character if you are not careful. Be thoughtful about what you say around children. Gone are the days when people thought it was acceptable to say the N-word. However, today common statements like "that is gay" or "he is a faggot" are not only demeaning but equally wrong. I hear these statements in the halls of my high school and at the checkout in the grocery store.

One of the most powerful speeches ever given was Dr. Martin Luther King's "I Have a Dream" speech. The following excerpt from that speech is posted in my classroom: "I have a dream that my four children will one day live in a nation where they will not be judged by the color of their skin but by the content of their character." When I am talking about his speech with my students, I always add, "I have a dream that one day we will live in a nation where nobody is judged by their race, religion, gender, size, or sexuality but by the content of their character."

Parenting at Our Best

Consider that when you make a racist or inappropriate joke, you teach your children to do the same and to treat others poorly.

When people find out I was a public defender, they often ask me how I could do it. I do not hesitate to say that everyone deserves to be represented, and it is such an important role in the judicial system. The system would not work without the defense attorneys. But when I look back on my short career as a deputy public defender, I can recall one of the most difficult cases. It was representing a nineteen-year-old young man who was a skinhead.

Skinheads are members of the Aryan Nation who believe in white superiority. He was in custody for damaging a black family's property. I really did not want to represent him, but as a public defender, I did not have a choice. I decided the only way I could do my job and feel good about it was to talk to him about why he felt the way he did. I think I sat in that tiny cell separated by glass with him for about two hours. It was one of the longest interviews I ever conducted.

I asked him why he did what he did and why he was a skinhead. He started babbling something righteously about how "those people take all our jobs from us." I came back with, "What job did you lose?" He said he had not actually experienced it firsthand but had heard about it. We talked for a long time, and I realized everything he spouted was what he had heard from others and none of what he had actually experienced himself. This hatred had come from listening to others vent their hatred. I, of course, tried with all my naive sprit to convince him otherwise.

In the end, I am sure he questioned my representation of him. But through that case, I came to realize how powerful hate was. He had not even experienced anything to cause him to feel such hatred. He was just surrounded by others and picked it up.

Be careful what you say around your children. Surround them with a good, positive environment. Don't spread hate.

Building Self-Esteem

The environment a child is raised in plays a huge factor in that child's life. If children live in fear each day that they will be put down or treated with anger every time they mess up, it takes away from their self-confidence. Kids already have that worry in school each day. They worry about answering questions wrong and looking stupid to the other kids. They need you to build them up at home so they can go out in the world confidently. If they live in a safe environment, they are free to be who they are meant to be.

One of the most important things you can do is to build and develop your children's self-esteem. They need to feel so good about themselves that they won't go along with the crowd when the crowd is doing bad things. Peer pressure can be very powerful, and to help your children make good decisions when you are not around, you must give them the confidence to stand up to the pressure and do the right thing. You need to encourage and nurture your children too. Give them self-confidence, but correct them carefully when they are wrong.

Tell them you believe in them and know they are good people also. Praise them when they do well. They need to hear that you are proud of them. One parent talked about the fact that she never felt good enough growing up. No matter what she did, she could not please her father, and her primary motivation through her childhood was trying to please him. Because of this, she never felt good enough, and as a parent, she told her children she was proud of them often. We all need to feel appreciated and believe that we are good enough.

Build your children up but remember to have balance. One parent remembered another parent who always told her child she was the best at everything. Even when the girl lost at something, her mother told her she was still the best. This parent thought that this was overboard and that giving too much praise can be unhealthy. Also, she felt the child may think she could never live up to this perfect image of being "the best" at everything. Instead, be genuine and authentic with your praise.

Creating a Respectful, Empathetic Child

Mutual respect is critical. If you demand respect from your children, you owe them respect. Children don't feel loved if they are not respected. Be careful what you do and say to your child so you do not lose that respect.

One of the first things a parent needs to do is establish a respectful relationship with your children at a young age so that it is there when they are going through the difficult teenage years. You can teach respect through your own relationship with your spouse. If you and your spouse treat each other with respect, your children will learn a lot from watching the two of you interact. This is also how they will learn to treat their spouses.

Teach them to respect their elders, but also be sure they know that it is all right to stand up for themselves. Show them how to respectfully question authority when they feel they are being wronged. Teach them humility by showing them that there are proper ways to get their views across without being disrespectful or boasting. If they make mistakes, show them how to own up to them. One parent showed his son the importance of respect by making him write a paper on respect after he punched a hole in the wall when he got angry.

Show your children how to have empathy for others as well. One parent did this by taking his son to poorer neighborhoods and showing him how others had to live. They even volunteered in the neighborhood so his son could see firsthand what the living conditions were like and how hard the people struggled. Another parent adopted a family in need through their church to teach their children this lesson.

Empathy for others is an important social skill—one you should work hard to refine in your children. You can teach empathy when your children make mistakes. Talk to them about how the other person might feel when they hurt someone. They need to understand their actions affected someone else and may have caused that person pain. Don't go too overboard, though, as children are fragile, and you don't want them to feel so bad they get depressed. One parent talked about the fact her daughter had so much empathy for others that all her friends came to her when they had problems. She was someone they could talk to and know she did not judge them.

Teach your children that when they are respectful, honest, good people, they get to do the things they want to do. Explain to them that you can give them more independence if you know they are trustworthy. By rewarding their good character, you boost their self-confidence and help them to become good people.

So many parents are so focused on how well their children do in school and whether they got an A that they miss out on an equally important if not more important factor than IQ called Social IQ. Daniel Goleman, author of the book *Social Intelligence: The New Science of Human Relationships*, explains the importance of Social IQ. He writes, "Empathy and social skills are the two main ingredients of social intelligence. This includes being able to read a situation to know how to make a good impression and being able to sense another's feelings and intentions."[xxii] He goes on to state that some businesses are even considering this in their hiring processes. Teaching your children empathy and good social skills will help them be successful.

While teaching the past eleven years, I have really seen how students are pressured to get good grades and be in advanced placement classes so that they can get into top colleges. The competition to get into certain colleges is extremely stressful and puts a lot of undue pressure on young people. The pressure has gotten so bad that cheating has become an acceptable practice to help alleviate some of the pressures.

Amy Novotney, the author of the article "Beat the Cheat," wrote, "More than half of teenagers say they have cheated on a test during the last year—and 34 percent have done it more than twice—according to a survey of 40,000 U.S. high school students released in February by the nonprofit Josephson Institute of Ethics. The survey also found that one in three students admitted they used the Internet to plagiarize an assignment." [xxiii]

I have been truly saddened by the fact students have become so willing to accept cheating as a means of getting ahead. I have had many discussions about this in my classroom, and I am shocked by many students' lack of integrity when it comes to cheating. It has almost become an acceptable practice to them.

I feel very strongly about this issue and try to relay the message that their character is more important to me than any grade they would get. But this message also needs to come from home. How many illegal financial scandals will it take before we realize we are not stressing the importance of honesty and integrity in the work a person does? Talk to your children about the importance of not cheating and stress that their integrity is more important to you than their grades. If your children have to cheat in order to get good grades, there are bigger problems to deal with. Deal with the problems, so they won't resort to cheating and compromising their spirits.

In closing it is important to remember, we are all different. Why can't we embrace that and teach our children not to be afraid of our differences but learn from them? You may not like the way others lead their lives and you would defiantly not lead yours in that way, but that does not give us the right to treat others badly.

Instead, teach your children to value all people. If we are going to judge people, judge them on their character, not how they look or who they choose to love. Imagine a world like that! I know the bullying issues in schools would decrease if we all worked toward that goal.

As parents, we hold the most influential role in helping our children have good character. Teach them that the packaging on the outside is not who they really are. They are so much more than their physical appearance. Their character, their spirit is the essence of who they really are. Nurture that!

Chapter 11 - Children Are Different

"Our greatest strength as a human race is our ability to acknowledge our differences, our greatest weakness is our failure to embrace them."[xxiv] *(Judith Henderson)*

You see the differences in children at birth. Some are easy babies who sleep and eat and require little else, while others can cry inconsolably and need a lot of attention. They may come out looking just like their big brothers and sisters, but they all have their idiosyncrasies.

Children are all different; therefore, they may require different parenting. You may not be able to be the same parent with each one. Let them be who they are. They don't all fit the molds we expect them to. You must accept them for who they are.

Allison Merkle Alison

How to Nurture Your Child as an Individual

All of us want our children to be successful and be the best they can be, but you must accept them for who they are in order for them to become their personal best. They may not be the top students in class, and that is fine. You want them to be well-rounded and happy. All you can expect is that they do their best. Just remember their best may be different from their siblings' best.

If you don't accept them for who they are, they won't feel good about themselves. They can't help the way they are, and you must love them no matter what. If you don't accept them, all of you will be miserable. There is one place everyone should be able to be himself; it should be home. Be tolerant of your children and make sure your home environment is a place where your children feel loved and accepted for who they are.

Remember that all children have strengths and gifts, so make sure to tell your children they are just as important and talented as anyone else. Be aware of their distinct personalities and the essence of who they are. Observe their likes and dislikes. Listen to what they say and try to be open and accepting of who they are as people.

When they mess up, you don't have to accept the behavior, but you must accept them. Value them and others. Help them to accept themselves for who they are. They each have their own strengths, and you need to point those strengths out in each of them.

There have been many books and articles written on the effects birth order has on children's personalities. Usually being the oldest forces a person to have to grow up quicker and be more responsible, but I also think parents' parenting styles may have something to do with this. Firstborn children are the guinea pigs. My mother often says, "There shouldn't be firstborn children."

She feels so bad for them, because new parents tend to overreact about everything. By the time the younger children come along, the parents have mellowed and seen that things do usually work out for the best and realize that overreacting does not help.

Children have different strengths and passions, so you need to allow them to pursue the activities they love, not just the ones the older sibling or parents did. Look at their strengths and steer them toward them. Really listen to what they like and guide them in those directions, even if you had other plans for them.

For example, one parent I interviewed talked about the fact that one of her daughters wanted to compete in beauty pageants. No one in her family had ever taken part in beauty competitions, and she did not particularly like the idea. She talked to her daughter about her concerns and eventually allowed her to do it.

It turned out the daughter was good at competing and won. Her daughter eventually figured out on her own that she did not want to make a career of the pageant industry, but the good thing was that the mother supported her daughter and let her figure things out on her own.

Another parent noticed that his son loved to play with LEGO sets when he was young, so he encouraged him to become an engineer. Today that son has his own company and is very successful.

One student relayed the story about her older sister who wanted to become a teacher, although their parents wanted her to become a doctor or lawyer because the parents saw these professions as highly regarded. Her sister did not give up her dream, and they constantly battled over it. It was exhausting for the whole family.

Eventually, she did become a teacher. Her parents saw how happy she was and accepted her, as well as her chosen profession. Today, she is very successful and a highly regarded teacher. She loves what she does and fought to have her own life. This was very tough on the family and, in hindsight, was not necessary.

Instead, get to know your children's passions and let them pursue them. Some children may take longer to figure out what they want to do with their lives. Give them time and allow them to mature. Remember, they don't all mature at the same time; instead, children are all individuals.

Also remember the importance of encouraging your children to do the things they are good at and enjoy doing, and if they can make a living out of it, help them pursue it.

Parenting Challenging Children

Some children are more challenging and require more assistance growing up. For example, one parent talked about the fact that when her children were young, the first child had been so easy but then the next one had allergies and another would not sleep through the night. She was exhausted attempting to meet the needs of all her children. The doctor told her to take a break and get a babysitter. She finally listened to him and took a break. She explained how important this advice and the break were to her, giving her a chance to restore her sanity.

Several parents talked about one child pushing their buttons more than the others, which forced them to adjust. One parent talked about the fact that each of her two children were challenging in different ways. Where one was very shy, the other was very outgoing. Each brought different challenges and required her to adjust. She was careful not to raise her voice with her shy son, but she knew she needed to raise her voice to deal with her rambunctious daughter.

Some children are just a little more rebellious than others too. One parent talked about her daughter who was much more challenging than her other two children. She refused to go to college when the time came and constantly went against the norm in the household. The mother realized she had to parent differently and convinced her daughter to at least participate in a leadership wilderness program. This allowed her to go away from home, grow up a little more, and appreciate all she had.

The daughter later went to college and eventually became an attorney. In the end, it all worked out, but the mother had to realize she could not change her daughter; instead, she had to change her parenting. She later looked back on it all and realized her older children had done so well in school that maybe her daughter had been a little intimidated and felt it was hard to live up to them at the time.

Another parent talked about her children and clearly stated the way she parented her daughter was different than her son because of who he was. She often had to say to him, "Could you please say that again in a nice voice, not in a mean one?"

Another parent tried very hard not to get upset by the fact that one of his children was nonverbal at two years old. He knew he couldn't compare him with his older siblings and needed to relax, knowing everything would work out, but it was difficult for him. He consciously let his son be who he was, and eventually he did talk. Unless you think your child suffers from some physical disability that is hindering their development, be careful not to compare milestones of each child because they all learn and develop at different rates.

One parent relayed the story about her younger son who had a more difficult time in elementary school than his two older siblings. She had never received a call from the school related to her older two children, but she did for the younger one. He was very social and outgoing, and it was hard for him to sit still in school. She even remembers having to yell at him. Her older daughter looked at her in shock, because she had never heard her mother yell before—she'd never needed to raise her voice with the older two.

What this mother finally realized was that she needed to change her parenting style to meet her son's needs. What she had done with the older two would not work for him. She read books and went to parenting classes to learn more about parenting a child like him. He went on to become very successful in school and even followed his siblings to the same college.

One student talked about the fact that his younger brother constantly argued with his parents, while he himself rarely argued with them. His parents needed to adjust to this and discipline his brother in such a way that he could learn to communicate more effectively.

No matter the troubles they present, you can never give up on those challenging children. You created these children, and they are your responsibility. You must find it in yourself to accept them and help them be the best they can be. It is hard, but be consistent and don't let your temper go or let them suck the life out of you.

In order to meet these goals, be sure to make time for yourself. You can't take care of your children until you take care of yourself. When they are little, it can be difficult because they rely so heavily on you, but just know it will get better as they get older and become more independent.

Balancing the Needs of All Children

Some children may require more of your attention, but all of your children need you. Be careful not to let one child's disabilities or needs take you away from your other children whose needs seem more easily met.

For example, one parent talked about the fact that one of her siblings had a disability and got all their parents' attention. She really wished her parents had taken a little more time with her while still meeting the needs of her disabled sibling. When this particular parent had a family of her own, she made sure to have special time with each child one-on-one. Her experience reminds us to try not to let the needs of one child keep us from meeting the needs of the others.

Another student of mine worked so hard at being perfect that he lost himself in the process. He had grown up in a family with a sibling who had a life-threatening medical issue, one she will have to fight her entire life. The parents rallied around that child and gave everything they had to her.

This student watched as his parents worried and consumed themselves with the disease his sister battled. His sister was the focus of the family unit. I am not judging these parents at all; in fact, I respect them for doing everything they could for their child. However, it was at the expense of their other child. My student was so determined not to cause any problems for his parents that he spent his life trying to be perfect at everything.

For example, he had to have the highest grades, be the best in music, be the best athlete, and be the most caring friend. He was seen as this amazing young person, but on the inside, he was suffering greatly. Eventually, the facade came down, and he had to get help. It was very painful and hard for him to let anyone know he was suffering, because he did not want to be a burden to his already burdened parents who, as he saw it, had enough to deal with.

If you are in this position and trying to balance the needs of your disabled or special needs child with your other children, once in awhile take the other children out by themselves and give them some one-on-one time. Don't just focus all your attention on the child with the disability or special need. Even in a family where none of the children have special needs, it's important to make each child feel special and spend one-on-one time with each of them. Everyone needs the attention. Make your children feel important both individually and collectively.

Be careful not to let the needs of one child destroy another. They all need attention, although some of them may not show it as visibly. If you are in this difficult situation, check in with your other children and make sure they are getting the attention they need. Also, remember to take care of yourself, so you can be strong enough to face these challenges head on.

Supporting Your Gay and Lesbian Children

As a history teacher, I have taught over and over again each year the history of discrimination against certain groups of people ranging from Native Americans to African Americans, Irish Americans, Italian Americans, Japanese Americans, Jewish Americans, Mexican Americans, and Muslim Americans. All this discrimination seems to be based in fear of the unknown. When we act in fear, we usually don't act well.

Today there is another group of people that is persecuted and demonized—the gay and lesbian community. This persecution is taking its toll on gay and lesbian Americans. According to a 1999 study using data collected among Massachusetts high school students in 1995, gay, lesbian, bisexual, and questioning high school students were more than three (3.41) times more likely to report having attempted suicide than their straight peers.[xxv] According to Suicide.org, an organization dedicated to the prevention of suicide, "Gay, lesbian, bisexual, and transgender teens are vulnerable to depression and suicide because they not only deal with the normal problems of being a teen, but also the discrimination, intolerance, harassment, and hate of people who cannot accept their orientation."[xxvi]

Over the years, I have listened while many young people poured their hearts and souls out to me about their struggle with their sexuality. I don't know if they come to me because I expect that in my classroom everyone is treated with respect or because I will point out to students who say "that's so gay" that they should use another phrase like "that is so silly." I think and hope all my students know that I won't tolerate anyone treating anyone else in my class with disrespect for any reason, so I often find myself as a listener to many teens struggling with this issue.

All I do is listen to the students and accept them. I don't judge them or condemn them in any way. What I have learned over my life is that being gay is just a part of who a person is, and you can't make someone stop being gay any more than you could make someone gay. I have always thought about it like this: I knew from a young age that I liked boys. You could not have done anything to me to make me like girls. I am attracted to boys. So, how can I expect a young man who is attracted to boys to be attracted to girls? It just does not work that way. As long as they are good, law-abiding citizens, who am I to judge, anyway?

One student I remember who was struggling with this issue was very upset because in his house he often heard derogatory remarks about others, such as "look at the faggot" or "don't act like a faggot." He was hearing all this as he was growing up and struggling with this issue. He clearly got the message that it was not okay to be who he was.

I can't imagine trying to grow up with all the pressures of the teenage years, trying to figure out your sexuality, and wondering if your family will accept you or reject you. As a parent, it is so important to not make derogatory remarks about gays or lesbians, because you don't know the struggles your children may face. Making those statements won't prevent your children from being gay. It will just let them know you don't accept them.

The other thing we all need to do as parents is to not be tolerant when other people say horrible things about gays or lesbians. When someone says "that is so gay," correct him or her politely and ask him or her to use another term like silly or strange.

Many of the parents I interviewed believed religion played an important role in helping their children learn values and respect. However, if you belong to a church that teaches followers that gay people are sinners or one that voices horrible messages about gays and lesbians, it may be doing more harm than good. Can you imagine being forced to go to a church that says you are evil for being who you are? I don't think that is what God or Jesus intended. That flies in the face of most religious teachings. Catholic priest Rev. John J. Unni said it the best: "'You are welcome here, gay or straight, rich or poor, young or old, black or white. . . . Here, you all can say, 'I can worship the God who made me as I am.'"[xxvii]

I truly believe people condemn others because they are afraid of what they don't understand. Educate yourself on the subject, and you will learn that gay and lesbian folks are people just like everyone else. I can't tell you the number of times I have heard from these struggling teens that they could not wait to be eighteen and go live somewhere where they would be accepted. If you don't accept your children for who they are, you will lose them. You will be missing out on being a part of this amazing person's life too.

Keeping It Positive

Whether we know it or not, our negative thoughts are felt by others. If your children constantly feel your disapproval, they react in a negative way. Change your thoughts about them and see what happens.

When your children are being difficult or rebellious or acting in a manner that does not meet your expectations, it is easy to get in the trap of focusing so much on their negative qualities that you can't even see the gifts they present. One technique I have tried to implement in my life is to make myself stop focusing on the negative qualities and instead focus on the positive ones. The more I focus on the positive qualities, the more positive I feel about the person. I change how I react to them and how I think about them, making a decision to focus on the positive and not on the negative.

The next time your children are acting out and driving you crazy, stop and think about the things you do like about them. I know this can be difficult in the teenage years, but try. Next time negative thoughts about them come to mind, replace them with positive thoughts. For example, if you have a teenager who never cleans her room, is always talking back, and refuses to listen, try to think of at least one thing or maybe several that she is doing well. She may be kind to her sibling or earning good grades at school. The next time you start thinking the negative thoughts, stop yourself and say in your head, "She is a good sibling and has really good grades." Continue to do this, and I think you will see an improvement in your relationship.

Remember too that you may have certain dreams and visions for your children, but they are who they are, not who you'd like them to be. Their lives may not turn out the way you envisioned them. They may not be the people you expected them to be. Their dreams may not be the same as yours. None of that matters; accept them and love them for who they authentically are. You play a huge role in their development, but at some point, you must accept the fact that they are who they are.

When they are young and you are so exhausted, remember that it will not always be that way. All parents need to remember that this too shall pass. Love all your children equally and make sure they know this. Try not to compare them. Who knows, they may just turn out to be the most interesting and creative people if all of you can just get through the challenging times.

Chapter 12 - Be Involved and Know Their Friends

"To be in your children's memories tomorrow, you have to be in their lives today." (Anonymous)

Ask any parents of grown children what they wished they had done more of when their children were young, and chances are they won't say they wished they had a cleaner house. They would most likely say that they wish they had been more present and spent more time with their children. Remember that what you give out is what you get back. If you are too busy in your work or social life to be with your children, you are teaching them how to act when they are older. Don't be surprised, then, when they are too busy for you and family time later on.

It is important to be involved in your children's lives while they are young. Create a home that is a place for them to feel welcomed and cared for, a place that will help them grow into the people they are meant to be. You can be "home" but not present, so it is important to remember to be an important presence in your children's lives. Really look at them when they talk to you. Really take the time to answer their questions and delight in their antics. Be present in the moment with them, because before you know it, the moments will be gone.

Supporting Your Children's Friendships

As a parent, I tried to make our house a place where my children felt they could invite their friends over and also a place where their friends would like to visit. We had a room set up in the basement with a movie area, pinball and ping-pong games, and no shortage of fun activities. I felt that if I wanted to make sure my children were in a safe environment with their friends, I had to provide one for them. Fortunately, many of my children's friends' homes were like that too.

It is important for your children to make friends and to have a home environment and parental encouragement to support their growing friendships. Friendship is an essential factor in life, with friends often operating just like family members in helping people grow into their full potential. Therefore, it is important for you to teach your children to make friends and choose them wisely.

Help your children learn how to make friends by providing rich opportunities for friendships to form. When children are young, encourage them to step up and take the plunge to make friends. What is the worst thing that can happen? Someone may say no? That's okay, because eventually someone will say yes, and your child will have made a friend.

Getting involved in activities is a great way to meet other children. Some children are shy by nature and may need pushing to put themselves out there. Another great way to encourage your children socially is to urge them to take more difficult classes in high school in order to surround themselves with higher achieving children who encourage them to excel.

It is important to encourage your children to make friends; those friendships help them learn how to socialize. My children grew up in a neighborhood with a lot of children on the block. Looking back now, I realize those children and their parents played a critical role in the development of my children. My parents always said to move into the best neighborhood you can afford for your children. Look at the schools and environment you place them in. I was very careful and fortunate to have found the neighborhood my children grew up in. However, it was not without a little drama.

I learned a valuable lesson early on to not get involved in the girl drama on the street in our neighborhood. I remember when my daughter was young and she came to me upset because she thought the girls on the block were being mean to her and excluding her. Now, most of their mothers were friends of mine, so this was a sensitive issue. She was really upset, though, and I, unfortunately, got caught up in the drama. I called several of the other mothers to try and work it out, and it almost seemed to make things worse. It seemed like everyone had had an issue at one time or another when her child felt left out too. After talking to them, I felt a little upset.

The next day, I was still upset over the whole exclusion issue. I looked outside, and my daughter was playing happily with her friends again, like everything was okay. What? They had, apparently, moved on from the drama, and she seemed just fine. I realized then and there that I would not ever get caught up in my children's friend drama again. I would listen to them, but I would not try and fix it. That was up to them.

It can be hard to watch your children suffer, especially if they feel they are being left out, but they must learn to deal with things on their own, just like my daughter did. You can listen and be there for them to help think of solutions, but they have to learn the social skills to nurture and develop friendships. Children will feel left out at some point; you have to help them see that it is not the end of the world and that they can resolve disputes. Show them that they have the power to improve the situation. Remember, you must be the parent and not the friend. Don't get involved in their little squabbles.

Friendship is particularly important in the teenage years. If a young person feels cut off and lonely, it may lead to depression. One parent talked about the fact that when her son messed up, it was actually his lifelong friends who were on him to get it together. Of course, it is usually the other way around, and parents are worried about the possible bad influences other children may have on their children.

If your children seem to be getting involved with the "wrong" crowd, get involved and be on top of the small stuff. Talk to them about these friends in a nonjudgmental way and try to help them see the importance of making good choices in friends. Tell your children that if they find themselves in difficult situations and are feeling pressured to do things they know are wrong to use you as their excuse. One parent told her daughter when she first started dating that she could always call her anytime to pick her up and to use her as the excuse to get out of a difficult situation. The mother told her daughter there would not be any ramifications, so she felt safe to call.

If your children feel they can talk to you about things and you will listen and not judge them, you will know more about what is going on in their lives and with their friends. Keep the lines of communication open, particularly in the teenage years. If you are concerned about a certain friendship, steer your child in another direction to get him away from the other child. Do things subtly so your child is not always with that particular friend. Also encourage him to hang out with children you think are doing well. You can even casually set up situations so they can hang out together. Some parents used their church to find friends for their children to hang out with in the hope they were hanging out with children of similar values.

Children can be very protective of their friends. They may even lie for them to protect them. Friendship can be a very strong and important relationship, so you have to be careful not to talk too harshly about friends. Even if your children come to you and tell you things about their friends in anger, you can't use that information against them the next time your children say they are getting together with the friend they'd been angry with. If you do that, you will shut down the lines of communication. In the end, remind your children to make good choices with their friends, but you can't use anything they've told you against them at a later time. Instead, give your children the opportunity to learn from life—and friends—and be there for them when they need you.

How to Get Involved in Their Lives and Encourage Healthy Development

If your children feel valued and know you are always there for them, they can grow up to be confident adults. Many of us have attended sporting events or band recitals when some parents did not show up for their children. We could truly see the hurt in the children's eyes and just wanted to give them a hug. When parents don't show up, they send the message that their children are not valued.

One parent who was a teacher and coach really stressed that parents' careers can't be more important than their children. When you become a parent, you have to let go of your selfish desires and put your children first, he explains. He was the head coach of a high school football team and decided he had to step down so he could be with his own children. He went on to say, "Don't spend your whole time raising someone else's children. Raise your own."

If your children like video games, play some games with them from time to time. That may just be the moment they open up to you. If they have an interest in baking, show them how. Do things together that they are interested in. Again, this shows your children that you value them. This is their world, and if you want to relate to them, you have to enter it.

When speaking to my students, I have learned that teens appreciate it when their parents take time to coach sports teams or lead activities related to them. These teens genuinely want their parents involved in their lives, because they like being with them. They have even commented, upon reflection, about their preschool and day care experiences, stressing that parents shouldn't worry if their children are in day care while they need to work, Parents just need to make sure they are fully engaged when they are home.

Kids also appreciate it when you know their friends and what they are doing, although they may not seem to like it. Children need their parents to keep them in check and to let them know when they are making good decisions—or bad ones. You can also introduce your children to and include them in your activities. In this way, they can be more involved and present in your life too.

Always be an important presence in your children's lives, no matter what. If you can't show up, get a grandparent or other relative to go in your place. Grandparents are a great resource to help out and can be an invaluable relationship for your child, but you must also have balance here. There is no substitute for a caring, involved parent, even with the best intentions of the grandparents.

Encouraging Kids' Sports Involvement

Another way you can encourage your children to make the right friends and learn social skills is to attend their sporting events or other activities and be their biggest supporter. One parent talked about the fact that her own parents had only attended the activities that they liked themselves and would not attend the activities she was in that they did not like. This hurt her, and as a parent, she made a conscious effort to attend all activities her children were involved in, regardless of her own pleasure. So, if you are a football-obsessed father, you not only have to support your son in football, but you also have to support your daughter in cheerleading or dance. This shows each of your children that you value him or her as an individual.

When your children are trying new sports or activities, it may be difficult at first. Be there to support them and encourage them to keep at it; sometimes they just need someone to push them to grow. But if they continue to be miserable and unhappy, it may be time to stop the activity.

One parent, who is also a coach, said that the parents on the team who were too controlling and involved made life difficult for him and their children. Just because your children are on the field does not mean you can coach them from the sidelines and scream demeaning comments. The coach, instead, really appreciated the parents who were present but stepped back and let him coach. Support your children, but don't yell at them and embarrass them from the sidelines.

Another parent learned a great way to interact with her children after the games. The school where her children attended encouraged the parents to do three things after a game: first, tell them you love them; second, tell them you enjoyed watching them play; and finally, ask them what they would like to eat. That's it, no recap or parental coaching.

Many children get burned out by the time they enter high school from over commitment to activities and sports when they were young. Be careful not to over commit your children in too many activities. Watch for signs of stress and make sure your kids are not taking their recreational pursuits so seriously that they are being affected in a negative manner.

How Healthy Involvement Can Ease Kids' Growing Pains (Or How Unhealthy Involvement Can Hinder It!)

When your children feel like they can talk to you about anything, you hear a lot of things you may not want to hear and that make you cringe. Just be glad you are in the loop and can maybe steer them in the right direction.

I remember a conversation with my daughter when she was in middle school that freaked me out. At that time in my life, I had already learned the PEER listening skills, so I really did listen to her. She proceeded to tell my about her thirteen-year-old friend who was having sex with her boyfriend. She was concerned about her and further told me her mother had put her on the pill. It was very difficult not to gasp out loud, and I did everything I could not to let my jaw fall to the ground.

As I was listening to her go on with the conversation, my head was screaming things like, "What? Thirteen and having sex?! What the hell?!" I was looking at this angelic thirteen-year-old child—my own daughter—and wondering, "Does she think this is okay? Will this happen to her?"

I am glad I kept quiet and composed, because, on her own, she said she thought it was wrong and a mistake on her friend's part. In fact, my daughter learned a lot from watching her friend make this mistake. She thought her friend was way too young to have sex and that it messed up her relationship with her boyfriend. She told me several times not to judge her friend or think badly about her, though.

We ended up having a really good discussion about sex and dating. I was proud of my daughter for not judging her friend and glad she came to me. But I knew I could never say anything derogatory about the girl in question. I also knew I could not prevent her from hanging out with the girl the following week when they wanted to get together. I nonchalantly encouraged them to come to our house to hang out so I could keep an eye on the situation. In the end, they drifted apart in high school and hung out in different circles.

It may be difficult, but when your children come to talk to you, try to just listen. Try not to judge and impart all your wisdom on them. It doesn't mean you can't interject a little every now and then, but they may just need to figure it out on their own, just like my daughter did.

It is also important to be involved and really know when something is bothering your child. One parent talked about the time his son was being bullied at school. He noticed he was a little sad and withdrawn, so he talked to him about it and tried to help him figure out a way to solve it.

Being there for your children when they go through difficult situations, like bullying, is so important. However, in this situation, when it continued and seemed to become more aggressive, the parent went to the school and talked to the teacher and guidance counselor. They brought all the boys involved together and worked it out. It was a teachable moment for all involved. It is important to let your children learn to handle things on their own, especially their relationships; however, if you feel your children are in danger or depressed, you need to intervene and get help.

But remember the balance, so you don't become too involved and become one of those "helicopter parents"—the ones who are always hovering too close to their children to allow for their children's healthy development. Be involved in their lives, but not too involved. Parenting is all about balance. Also, remember to be the parent and not a friend. Children—particularly teenagers—need their parents to parent and not to be their friends. You certainly can be friendly toward them, but you must be the adult in the relationship. When they are older and grown, you can be their friend.

When children start going to friends' homes, remember that it is okay to call the parents at the home where they will be, but don't go overboard and spy on them. Most parents appreciate the call and will think more highly of you and your children. Don't interfere so much that you break your children's trust, though. They need to feel you trust them. If they end up breaking your trust, then there should be consequences, and they will have to earn the trust back. It is all part of growing up and learning.

In the high school years, however, there was the home where, rumor had it, the parents allowed children to drink alcohol. As an attorney, I know the criminal and civil ramifications of giving alcohol to minors and would never provide alcohol to anyone else's underage child. I am not saying I have never allowed my own children to drink alcohol in my home underage, but that is very different than allowing another person's child to drink. It was very frustrating that these parents let these children drink in their home. It not only created problems for the rest of us parents, but it also sent the wrong message to the young people present. These parents were so busy trying to be cool and be friends to their child that they forgot they needed to parent.

Think very carefully before allowing minors to drink alcohol in your home. You can be prosecuted criminally for contributing to the delinquency of a minor, and you can be sued civilly for money damages if something you did goes wrong. You are exposing yourself to serious consequences. Instead, let your home be a positive, safe environment where your children can bring their friends.

Again let me reiterate, don't fall into the trap of the situation where your child is asking to do something you feel very uncomfortable with and he says, "But Mike's parents are letting him do it." Call Mike's parents and see if this is true, and maybe talking to them will help you make a more informed decision. Don't just allow them to do things because you think other parents are allowing it. Chances are they are saying the same thing to their parents about you. If you suspect your child is doing inappropriate things, you must get involved. You cannot hide your head in the sand and hope it all goes away.

In the end, don't be so worried about cleaning the house or getting the laundry done. Instead, spend quality time with your children. And although your children's lives should be your main focus, that doesn't mean you can't and shouldn't have a life of your own. Again, it is about balance. It is great to have a hobby like golf, but when your children are young, you may not be able to play as much. Your family should be the priority in your life. When your children are grown—and the time will go fast—you can play all the golf you want.

Being involved in your children's lives does not end when they turn eighteen, though. Hopefully, they will need you a little forever. When they are older, you must give them the space to be independent young people, but you can do things nonchalantly to help them out. One dad talked about how he asked his twenty-five-year-old daughter to borrow her car. What he was really doing was taking it in to get checked, and he filled it with gas. He wanted her to know in a nonthreatening way that he was still there for her, even though she was all grown up. Remember that what you put out, you will get back when they are older. Help create children you will want to hang out with and enjoy.

Chapter 13 - Parents on the Same Page and Divorce

"The thing that experts agree on is that although divorce is difficult and stressful for kids no matter what, the real harm to kids comes from being subjected to conflict between parents. The longer that lasts, and the more severe it is, the worse it is for your children. If you truly want to shield your children from the pain of divorce, recognize that the more you take the high road with your spouse, the better job you'll do."[xxviii] *(Emily Doskow)*

Parents need to be on the same page when parenting their children, whether the parents never married, are divorced or separated, or are still committed to the marriage. If one parent is the bad guy and the other the good guy, it can tear a family—and thus the children—apart.

Parents also need to support each other in the caretaking duties of their children, no matter the condition of their own romantic relationship. Child rearing is not a female or male role; it is essential to encourage each other to be part of all the duties involved in raising your children.

Nurturing Sibling Relationships and Keeping Them Respectful

Fostering the sibling relationship is important to the children and family unit, so make sure both you and the kids' co-parent are on the same page. Sibling relationships are the first and longest relationships of most of our lives. Do your part to encourage that connection between your children.

One parent who was the parent of three boys explained how she handled sibling disputes. When her sons were fighting, she did not get involved but made them work things out themselves. They had to sit down in a room and talk it out—no punching allowed. They were not allowed to do anything else until they worked it out. She felt that if she had disciplined them for fighting by sending them to separate rooms, they would not have worked out their problems. She did not want to become the referee in the fight. She wanted them to learn how to solve issues.

She said that one time the boys came out of the room pretending like they had worked it out, because there was an activity they wanted to get to. She could tell they were still angry at each other, so she sent them back to work it out. Today these brothers are very close and support each other in their lives.

Sibling relationships help your children grow. Be sure to encourage healthy relationships that are based on respect. There will always be sibling disputes and rivalries, but make sure your kids learn to work it out themselves. Don't get drawn into the fights by taking sides, and don't become the fixer. Instead, teach your children to communicate respectfully and work it out, stepping in only if they are hurting each other. These are teachable moments that will help your children become adults who can handle conflict as they deal with other people and strife in their relationships.

Modeling Respect by Respecting Your Spouse

The relationship in your marriage is much like the relationship with your children. Good marriages take commitment and energy; they need to be respectful and nurturing. If you expect your children to respect you and others, you must demonstrate this by respecting your spouse. Your relationship with your spouse is the model they watch every day.

As such, be careful not to belittle each other or be demeaning. Remember that you are the role model for your children's relationships; how you treat your spouse is how they will expect to be treated in relationships and how they will treat others. Be sure, then, to nurture your relationship with your spouse so you remain a strong couple. You not only work on your marriage for yourself, but also for your children.

To keep your marriage thriving, be sure to carve out time for date nights and time alone together. Your children are your main focus, especially when they are little, but you must continue to nurture your marriage. Your children want you and your spouse to be happy as a couple and keep the family together. Make sure you carve out time to talk and connect as a couple in order to nurture this important relationship.

If you let your relationship with your spouse go and do not protect it, you may tear the family part. Being on the same page and connecting with each other is so important to a marriage. Remember that your children need and want both parents in their lives if possible, so make your own marriage a priority for the sake of the whole family.

Allison Merkle Alison

Parenting as Partners

Parenting, at its best, features teamwork, so be united as parents. Don't have one person be the mean one and one the nice one. Kids know how to divide you to get what they want, even though they also know this can cause trouble. Be together and act as a unified force, so kids cannot divide and conquer.

This can be difficult sometimes for mothers of young infants. Be careful not to criticize your spouse for not doing things a certain way. As long as the children are getting their needs met and are happy, it does not matter if their outfits are on backward. Instead, be gentle with your criticism and help your spouse be the best parent he can be. Encourage your spouse to participate in the daily duties, even if he does it wrong. Support each other, and your children will benefit.

Again, don't let these words pass your mouth either: "Wait until your father gets home." If inappropriate behavior occurred and consequences are necessary, you should take care of it yourself unless it is such a big issue that you need to discuss it with your spouse first. Don't make Dad the bad guy; it is essential to support each other in parenting our children.

If you and your partner have a disagreement over a certain parenting issue, don't let your children know. Talk about this in private away from your children until you resolve the issue. This is particularly essential in the teenage years. As children get older and wiser, they learn how to play one parent off of the other. Don't get caught in that trap. When your children know you and your husband are a unit, they learn they can't divide you.

One parent, who is a special education teacher and dean, could pick out in most parental meetings at his school who was the hard parent and who was the easy parent. He was shocked at how often the parents were not on the same page with regard to their children. He felt this was a huge mistake many parents made in the raising of children. He and his wife were older when they had their daughter and always talked about the issues involving her together. If there was disagreement over their daughter, they discussed it in private.

Another parent reiterated this same point and explained that she and her husband were raised in completely different households. As a result, they did not always agree on the some parenting styles. Importantly, though, they did agree that any issues they had would be talked about away from their children.

One couple, who were older parents by the time their son was born, talked about a lot of the parenting issues before the birth of their child. They talked about how they would handle certain situations, particularly discipline. The husband had been raised in a home with corporal punishment, but his wife had not. He agreed with her to not use corporal punishment, but he did want to make sure there were consequences for bad behavior and that those consequences were immediate. They agreed on using time-outs, which worked. Talking about this issue ahead of time helped build the parenting bond between them and made them a unit. When things occurred that they had not discussed, they would tell their son they had not thought about that issue and would talk about it and get back to him.

Be careful not to let your children play each of you when it comes to disciplinary issues. For example, when your child becomes a teenager, be sure to discuss critical issues like curfew, car privileges, and school expectations with your spouse. You don't want to continually hear, "But Dad said I could do it."

Try not to second-guess each other either. Instead, stand as a united front when it comes to parenting. For example, if your teenager wants to attend a party, come together as a couple to talk about it and set down the expectations you both agree with.

Being united does not mean you can't listen to your child's input on critical issues; it just means you and your spouse are united on the decision.

Also, each spouse should encourage the healthy potential relationship each parent could and should have with the children. In the difficult teenage years, one parent may be helpful in diffusing some issues for the other parent. One parent talked about the fact that his wife and daughter had a lot of disagreements when she was a teenager. He became the mediator between them and helped the relationship evolve. He was careful to always support his wife but to listen to his daughter's concerns also.

When my oldest daughter was born, I talked to my husband about how his relationship with her would play a pivotal role in her life. He had come from a long line of males filled with brothers and male cousins, and having a female in the mix was a new thing. I knew from my own relationship with my father how important it was.

See, my father always treated me with love and respect. I can remember waking up in the morning feeling like I looked like Frankenstein, and he would say, "Good morning, Beautiful." Of course, I rolled my eyes, but I grew up with positive messages from my dad like that one.

As a result, I was so confident about myself that in any relationship with a male I would never have allowed someone to treat me any other way than with love and respect. I just would not have put up with it. My father had taught me what to expect. I think watching my parents' healthy relationship and my confident mother also helped. My father had the upmost love and respect for Mom, as well.

My husband, being the amazing man that he is, really listened and has helped solidify that same confidence in our daughters. We often focus on the mother/daughter or father/son relationships when, in fact, the father/daughter or mother/son relationship may be more crucial. You must foster those bonds. Carve out special time for those relationships to build. Be the example for their future relationships.

Sadly, one parent talked about the fact that she and her husband got divorced for several reasons, one of them being the fact he thought she was too easy on the children and they did not find common ground on issues related to the kids. He always felt like he had to be the disciplinarian and "the bad guy." They just did not see eye to eye on the raising of their children, and it took its toll on the relationship.

As parents, if you have issues with each other's parenting style, sit down together away from the children and work it out. If you can't agree, you may need to seek professionals to help you work it out.

Also, if you are in a relationship that is physically or emotionally abusive, you are hurting your children and need to get help. Your children are forever scarred when they witness such abuse, because it is scary and stressful for them. If you and your spouse are not able to communicate without screaming at each other and becoming violent, you owe it to your children to get help. It is okay to have disagreements in a healthy manner and then show your children how to resolve them, but violence is never okay.

If you are in an abusive situation, you need to get help. Staying in an abusive relationship teaches your children that this type of behavior is acceptable. They are watching and learning from you. For example, if your husband is abusing you, you may be teaching your son to perpetuate that behavior and teaching your daughter that it is okay to accept that behavior. They, in all likelihood, will continue the cycle of abuse in their future relationships, because children live what they know.

As an attorney, I have watched this cycle repeat itself in the courts for years. If you find yourself caught up in this pattern of abuse, get help for the family or get out. There are women's shelters all over the country to help women in abusive situations. You do not have to remain in the relationship, and you owe it to your children to leave if it can't be fixed. As a parent, you have a duty to protect your children from violence, even it is from one of their own parents. Violence is not love. Even though divorce will cause pain for your children, the violence they are witnessing is far worse for them. They can survive the divorce and learn from it.

Staying on the Same Page after a Divorce

Divorce is difficult on everyone involved, especially the children. One parent relayed the statement her eight-year-old nephew made after his parents divorced when asked what he wanted for Christmas. He said, "All I want for Christmas is my family in our house."

Although divorce may be the only alternative in some situations, make no mistake—it will be hard on your children. You are breaking up the family. However, the trauma can be diminished significantly if you and your spouse remain civil during the process and throughout your children's lives.

One of the reasons I left the legal professions and became a teacher was because I just could not handle another nasty divorce case. I was often appointed to represent the children in a bad divorce. It was like the judge would appoint me as a last resort in these awful battles. My job was to figure out what was going on in this very dysfunctional family and what should happen to the children. Both sides would be saying horrible things about the other, and it was so difficult to know what was true. I had to do my best not to be pulled into either side's vendetta and really decide what was in the best interest of the minors involved. When researching these cases and meeting the families, I felt so bad for the children involved. They were so torn and confused. Usually all they wanted was their family back together and their parents to stop arguing.

If you feel that getting a divorce is the best solution to a very volatile and dysfunctional marriage, it doesn't do any good if you continue the same behavior with your ex-spouse after the divorce. Continuing to make disparaging remarks about a parent is upsetting to your children. Whether you want to face it or not, that person is their parent and plays a significant role in your children's lives. Talking badly about him and preventing him from seeing your children will only make them resent you in the end. Unless that parent is a real danger to your children, he should be involved in their lives.

In my experiences with teens, I have learned how a divorce can destroy a family and cause harm to the children. It hurts them so much; they may even start acting out. Some of them also seem to have trouble in their own relationships.

Children do not usually want their parents to divorce. Don't make the situation worse by making it a nasty divorce. You must think of the children first. You need to put your personal issues aside and take care of your children. They are hurting and need your support.

One of the best experts I have ever heard on this subject is M. Gary Neuman. He is the author of several books on relationships, including one titled *Helping Your Kids Cope with Divorce the Sandcastles Way*. Neuman has appeared on such shows as *Oprah* to talk about the harmful effects of divorce on children and what parents can do to protect them. He was very clear that children need to understand that the divorce was not their fault in any way. They need to have someone to talk to about their feelings and express their emotions. That person does not have to have all the answers but just be able to listen. He really stressed that children will not be okay unless you listen to them, reiterating the fact that listening to your children makes them feel valued.[xxix]

Furthermore, he reminded single parents that family is not just biology and that many other people can fill that missing role, including extended family members or neighbors. He also really stressed the importance of parents showing up at scheduled visitation times. When you don't show up, he explained, your children take it personally. He went on to say that children believe whatever messages you send to them and that they will make it through a divorce if you listen and care for them. This is how you show them you love them.[xxx]

One of the parents who came from a divorced family really respected her mother who took on the primary caretaking role after their father left the home and always encouraged her children to respect their father. Her mother did not talk badly about him and also expected the children to be respectful. She looks back on the divorce now as an adult and appreciates the fact her mother acted that way. It is hard enough to go through the breakup of the family without also having to continuing to endure the anger and resentment between the adults.

One parent had two siblings who were both divorced parents, and by watching them, she was able to see the importance of parents being on the same page even in a divorce situation. Her sister was divorced, but the sister and her ex-husband talked about parenting issues and supported each other. They even came to family events together and made sure not to fight in front of the children.

On the other hand, while the sister's children seemed to adjust much better because of teamwork, her brother's children did not adjust well because of a lack of teamwork. The brother and his ex-wife were constantly bickering and not on the same page when it

Parenting at Our Best

came to parenting. The children knew this and took advantage of the situation, pitting one parent against the other to get things they wanted. They knew just how to get their way and were out of control. Both parents were so busy fighting with each other that they could not parent their children. It is essential for divorced parents to put aside their differences and come together to parent their children, as illustrated by this scenario.

Another parent was very concerned for her nephew, who went through a difficult divorce when his parents split. He seemed so lost and alone. He always seemed to be torn apart over the fact that he did not know where his loyalties should be on issues in the family. The divorce was so contentious and antagonistic that he felt miserable and just seemed to be trying to get through life without any real joy. These parents, she explained, needed to put their son's needs first and stop only thinking about themselves. Even if their marriage did not work, they still had a child together who deserved parents acting appropriately and nurturing his development. The marriage ended, not the relationships.

One parent whose children are now very successful people got a divorce when her children were young. It was difficult on her and the children. At first, all she wanted to do after the divorce was lay in bed all day. However, she knew she could not do that, and she picked herself up for her children. She realized her children needed her at that time more than ever and devoted herself to them.

Although the circumstances of the divorce were painful for her, she did not drag her husband down either. She did not talk badly about him. Children do not want to hear bad things about either parent. When her youngest graduated, he said to her, "I always knew I had a mom and dad who loved me."

Don't let your pain and anger with your spouse spill over to your children. If you can be civil and join together in the raising of your children, your children will have a much better chance to adjust and become successful children, teens, and adults. This parent's biggest concern was how her children would learn what a good relationship was. But when she thought about it, she realized her own parents were a great role model for them in their lengthy and healthy relationship, and that comforted her.

When we pick the students that will be in the PEER group of counselors at our school, we put them through a rigorous selection process. On the application, they are asked to write about a difficult time or experience in their lives and how it affected them.

Over the years, a substantial number of students have talked about their parents' divorces as that challenge. They write about how tough it was on them, but many of them have said that going through the experience did make them stronger people. Some of the things they wished their parents had done better, though, were to be honest with them about what was going on, to not be too quick to bring a new person into their lives, and to remember that even if a new person does come into the picture, their loyalty resides with the other parent.

The best thing you can do for your children when going through a divorce is be there for them and listen when they need to express their feelings. Whether they are angry, sad, or depressed about the situation, they need to walk through the pain. Repressing it only leads to other problems later on. Your children can get through this if you make their needs a top priority and you are there for them.

Avoiding Isolation and Reaching Out for Support

One parent who was a social worker said that many of the families she investigated involved mothers who were isolated and cut off. As a result, the parent felt social interaction was essential.

Some difficulties come into play when one parent is the primary caretaker while the other parent is out making money or even living in another state, as in the case of divorce. Being an at-home parent can be one of the most difficult jobs. It is very important to set up some kind of support system for yourself, particularly when the children are young. If you don't have some kind of support, you can feel isolated and alone. This may even lead to issues in your marriage (if it is intact) and depression.

If you are home all day with your children, be sure to set up playdates with other parents and their children. One of the best support systems is playgroups that meet regularly. These outings allow your children to play with other children and give you an opportunity to talk to other parents about concerns or issues you may be facing as a parent. I know from my own experience how important this outlet can be for a stay-at-home parent.

I was fortunate to have a playgroup that met weekly at alternate homes when my children were young. It was truly a lifesaver for me not only because it gave me the social outlet I was craving but we shared parental advice and supported each other. We quite literally helped raise each other's children, and I am forever indebted to this amazing group of women. We started as a group of women in the neighborhood who got together for coffee, and it evolved into a group of amazing women from many different places and experiences. The funny thing is that seventeen years later, they still have playgroup one day a week even though most of the children are grown, and I join them on nightly events as the working mom.

One parent I interviewed talked about how parents in her neighborhood set up a babysitting group where they each took turns babysitting each other's children, giving each parent a little personal time. It was easy to set up, and one person volunteered to be the secretary for the group to keep the hours so they were fair. She felt this interaction was essential for both the children and the parents.

There are also programs like Big Brothers/Big Sisters in communities that will match your child up with a mentor. There are also counseling groups set up through the schools to deal with many different issues. Ask the guidance counselor at your children's school for help to find one that fits your family's needs.

Just remember that you don't have to do it alone, whether single, married, separated, or divorced. Take advantage of the resources out there. It is essential to get some personal time; otherwise, you feel like you are on duty 24/7. Don't be ashamed or hesitant to get a babysitter to help out. And, for the sake of your family, strive to maintain and encourage healthy relationships among all family members.

Chapter 14 - Love and Enjoy Your Children

"If you want your children to improve, let them overhear the nice things you say about them to others."[xxxi] *(Haim Ginott)*

How do you look and act when your children walk into the room? This statement is so powerful. Think about how you react when your children walk into the room or when you see them for the first time after being away from them. Are you so tired from the day at work that you don't even give them a smile?

When you introduce them to others, what words of praise do you use? And when they walk in the room, do you criticize them and focus on their negatives, or do you just look at them with loving pride and smile?

One of my favorite Oprah shows was when Nobel Prize-winning author Toni Morrison was on and she asked this question of all parents: "when your child walks in the room, does your face light up?" She went on to say, "When my children used to walk in the room when they were little, I looked at them to see if they had buckled their trousers or if their hair was combed or if their socks were up." She further said, "You think your affection and your deep love is on display because you're caring for them. It's not. When they see you, they see the critical face. But if you let your face speak what's in your heart … because when they walked in the room, I was glad to see them. It's just as small as that, you see." [xxxii]

I know that when my own children walk into the room, my whole body usually lights up, and I hope they see that. I know I am smiling, because I am truly happy to see them. I am not talking about when we are all in the house together; I am talking about when we are apart and have come back together or when I am introducing them to someone.

I remember when I had to leave my children to go to work or when I had to drop them off at preschool; it was often difficult to leave them. But when I got home or went to pick them up from school, I was so excited, and I know I lit up when I saw them. They, in response, would light up too. It made the being away from them bearable.

The significance of this is even greater now that they are older and off in college. I leap out of my skin when I see them after they have been away for a long time.

Again, I ask: what do your children see when you look at them? What do they hear in the words you tell them? What are your actions showing them about how you feel?

Communicating Your Love through Your Words and Messages

You should love your children unconditionally. That means you love them no matter what, and you accept them for who they truly are. Tell them you love them often. Make it known to them that you love them. It is so important for them to hear these messages.

Many of the parents I interviewed did not hear "I love you" from their own parents while growing up, and they desperately wanted to hear it. They made a conscious effort to tell their children this important message, perhaps even more so because they may not have heard it enough themselves. One parent I spoke with explained how she always closed conversations with her children by saying, "I love you," to make sure her kids always knew how she felt about them.

The words "I love you" are so powerful and important to say and hear. I don't think you can ever say those words too often to your children. I made a conscious effort to tell my children as often as possible these three beautiful words as they were growing up. And since what you give out you get back, I hear those words from my children all the time, although I did hear them less during the difficult teenage periods, I must admit.

I never get tired of hearing my children say those words. Just about every phone conversation ends with one of us telling the other those words. When we will be apart for any significant length of time, we always part on those words. We can't say them enough, and every time I say them or hear them, I smile. In my other relationships, saying those words so often may get old or disingenuous but not with my children.

I even came up with a secret hand squeeze when they were young, so I could relay that message at times when I could not talk to them. I would grab a hand and squeeze it three times, sounding out "I love you" in my head. I had taught them the meaning of the secret squeeze, so when I would do it, they would turn, look at me, and smile and always return the message. It came in handy in some difficult times.

Also, when our children were in elementary school, my husband and I would often put messages saying how much we loved them or telling them to have a nice day in their lunch bags. When they opened their lunch at school, there was a positive, loving message reminding them that we loved them. School can be stressful, and a little message can go a long way. Be creative in your reminders and the way you express your love. It can be a powerful way to build up your children.

Give your children lots of hugs and kisses! It is important to say the words "I love you," but it is also important to demonstrate love through your daily interactions. One of the best ways to demonstrate love is through respect. Remind your children that you will always be there for them no matter what.

Showing Your Love through Your Actions

When I first started conducting interviews with parents, I imagined that when I asked the first question ("What is one thing or maybe several things you would want to tell a new parent about parenting?") that everyone would say, "Tell them you love them." But it was not what I heard the majority of the time. Sure, the parents usually talked about it at some point in the interview, but it was not the first thing they usually said. It was all the other things talked about in this book previously that they felt were so important. I know they thought the words were important, but it was through providing the previous things that they really showed their love. They reinforced the message that a parent must parent. Parenting can be exhausting and challenging, but that is what you do when you love someone, they explained.

Although the words "I love you" are important to say, it is the demonstrations of love in their daily lives that will make your children truly feel loved. You can say "I love you," but if you do not nurture and care for your children, they will not feel loved.

The greatest gift you can give your children is the ability to love themselves. They need to love themselves for who they are, their strengths and their weaknesses, the good and the bad. I am not talking about being conceited or boastful. I am talking about being able to love themselves so that no matter what happens in their lives or what someone says about them, they will know they are good enough. I would like to say that I have always known this and that I knew to teach my children this as they were growing up, but I did not know the significance of loving oneself until later in life. I wish I had understood this when my children first came into my life.

Don't just love your children, but also like them. Enjoy hanging out with your children. Laugh a lot! Have fun! Don't be so busy that you wake up one day and realize your children are all grown and you were not present for their lives. Take time to play with them. Say yes more often and no less often. When you have fun with your children and laugh with them, you teach them to have a sense of humor.

Play lots of music in your house and make it a place they are happy to be. For example, one parent liked to put on music and dance around the house with her children. Another one did the same thing and used tennis racquets as guitars. They were the band, rocking out with their racquets.

One of the funniest memories I have of my husband was when he would put Phil Collins' *Tarzan* music on and chase the kids around acting like a big gorilla. They would laugh and squeal in delight as he chased them. The funny thing was that when their friends would come over, they would make him do it with all of them, saying, "Oh, Dad, be the gorilla and chase us around!" And, of course, he gladly would.

Another parent I interviewed loved playing with his children, just like my husband did. He played card games and word games; he told them stories and just really enjoyed his children. When he talked about the fun he had, tears welled up in his eyes because he truly enjoyed his children and treasured those memories. When you play with your children, you develop a bond with them. That bond will get you through the tougher times. Love and attention are the keys to that strong bond.

Do fun things as a family and spend one-on-one time with each child too. It does not have to cost money. Lay down in the grass with them and play, "What's in the clouds?" Just lay with them and let them tell you the things they see in the clouds.

Some of the parents I spoke to are grandparents and have gotten to spend more time with their grandchildren and enjoy them more than they did their own children. With their own children, they were so busy doing the mundane things that they missed the time with them. Now as grandparents, all they want to do is sit and talk to these precious children and grandchildren. They cherish the time they have with them. Stop what you are doing and don't worry about whether or not the dishes get done. Spend time with your children. They will be grown and gone before you know it.

Getting Help so You Can Love Your Children Fully

Throughout my years as a practicing attorney, I saw many drug- and alcohol-addicted mothers and fathers say "I love you" to their children in the courtroom, but their actions did not demonstrate that feeling of love. Many were so addicted to drugs or alcohol that they could not truly love anyone, including themselves. They seemed to be in love with the addiction. If you suffer from some form of addiction, get help. You owe it to yourself and your children.

Parenting at Our Best

There are also other addictions that keep you from your children, like being a workaholic, a gambler, or other addictive identities. These are all mental health issues that you should get help for. Finally, if you suffer from depression or other mental illnesses, you need to get professional help. You can still be a great parent, but you must get help. Show your love by making yourself the best person you can be for your children.

In closing, remember to have fun with your children! Some of my greatest memories of my children growing up are when we were acting goofy and laughing. I can remember putting on music while I made dinner, and as we waited for my husband to come home, we would all dance around and sing. We would even use the spatulas as microphones. Also, dinner has always been important to me because it is when we connect, but it is also when we laugh together and act so goofy. I could sit for hours and just laugh with my children—even today.

Try not to let the little things get to you and be more laid back. It will all work out. Don't get so upset about things. Be calm and don't take things so personally. Have a sense of humor about things. Many of us wish we had relaxed more and not been so uptight.

Take a deep breath! Don't be so worried about how things may look to others. Try not to be so serious. Laughter really is the best medicine, so have fun and enjoy your children because before you know, it they will be grown up raising their own families.

Conclusion

I really hope this book helps you in your parenting endeavor, but I also have a dream that it will open up the discussion for everyone. I think it is time for all of us to help each other be the best parents we can be. Leaving parents to their own devices and experiences does not make sense. There are some amazing parents who have survived the child-rearing experience and have some incredible advice and wisdom to share with others. I would like to see television shows dedicated to and focused on good parenting skills so that all parents have access to information that can help them be the best parents for their children. When children are raised in a functioning and loving family, we all benefit. I would like to see education and information available to all parents to be their best. When the parents, schools, and community are all working together for the benefit of the children, they can grow into the people they are meant to be.

Bibliography

Angelou, Maya. "Mothers: The 5 Questions You Need To Ask Yourself". *The Oprah Magazine*. September 2004. Print.

Brazleton, T. Berry and Joshua D. Sparrow. *Discipline: The Brazelton Way*. Cambridge, MA: Perseus, 2003. Print.

"Career Center Article". *Berkeley Web*. N.d. Web. 18 June 2012.

Caruso, Kevin. "Teen Suicide and Youth Suicide." *Suicide Prevention, Suicide Awareness, Suicide Support*. N.p., n.d. Web. 19 June 2012.

"Children of Alcoholics." *American Academy of Child & Adolescent Psychiatry*. Dec. 2011. Web. 18 June 2012.

"Children of Incarcerated Parents." *Oregon Department of Corrections*. N.d. Web. 18 June 2012.

Doskow, Emily. *Nolo's Essential Guide to Divorce*. Nolo. 2012. Print.

Fiese, Barbara H., Thomas J. Tomcho, Michael Douglas, Kimberly Josephs, Scott Poltrock, and Tim Baker. "A Review of 50 Years of Research on Naturally Occurring Family

Routines and Rituals: Cause for Celebration?" *Journal of Family Psychology* 16.4 (2002): 381-90. Print.

Friedman, Thomas. "How about Better Parents?" *NY Times*. 20 Nov. 2011. Web. 12 June 2012.

Fulghum, Robert. *All I Really Need to Know I Learned in Kindergarten*. New York: Villard, 1988. Print.

Garofalo, Wolf R. "Sexual Orientation and Risk of Suicide Attempts among a Representative Sample of Youth." *Pediatric Adolescent Medicine* (1999): 487-93. Print.

Gibbs, Nancy. "The Magic of the Family Meal." *Time* 04 June 2006. Web. 18 June 2012.

Ginott, Haim. *Between Parent and Child: The Bestselling Classic That Revolutionized Parent-Child Communication*. New York: Three Rivers, 2003. Print.

Goleman, Daniel. *Social Intelligence: The New Science of Human Relationships*. New York: Bantam, 2006. Print.

Henderson, Judith. "Judith Henderson quotes". ThinkExist.com Quotations Online 1 Jul. 2012 Web 22 Aug. 2012.

Josephson, Michael. "The Six Pillars of Character." *Josephson Institute Center for Youth Ethics*. N.p., n.d. Web. 18 June 2012.

Kahn, Ada P. *Encyclopedia of Mental Health*. New York: Facts on File, 2001. 438. Print.

Koch, Wendy. "Record Number of Foster Kids Leave Program as Adults." *USA Today*. 23 May 200. Web 18 June 2012.

Mandela, Nelson. "Nelson Mandela quotes". ThinkExist.com Quotations Online 1 Jul. 2012. Web 21 Aug. 2012.

Marston, Stephanie. *The Magic of Encouragement*. New York: Pocket, 1992. Print.

Morrison, Toni. "Oprah." *Oprah's Most Memorable Guests: the Greatest Lessons on the Oprah Show*. ABC. Chicago, Illinois, 13 May 2011. Television.

Neirfert, Marianne E. *Dr. Mom's Parenting Guide: Common-Sense Guidance for the Life of your Child*. New York: Plume, 1996. Print.

Nelson, Laura J. "Priest Says All Are Welcome in His Church." *The Boston Globe* 13 June 2011. Print.

Neite, Dorothy Law. "Children Learn What They Live." *100 Ways to Enhance Self-Concept in the Classroom: A Handbook for Teachers and Parents*. Boston: Allyn & Bacon, 1976. Print.

Neuman, M. Gary., and Patricia Romanowski Bashe. *Helping Your Kids Cope with Divorce the Sandcastles Way*. New York: Times, 1998. Print.

Neuman, M. Gary. "Oprah." *Adult Children of Divorce Confront Parents*. ABC. Chicago, IL, 01 Jan. 2006. Television.

Novotney, Amy. "Beat the Cheat." *American Psychological Association*. N.p., June 2011. Web. 18 June 2012.

Schwarz, Joel. "Children Whose Parents Smoked Are Twice as Likely to Begin Smoking between 13 and 21." *Medical News Today*. N.p., 01 Oct. 2005. Web. 18 June 2012.

Swindoll, Charles R. *The Strong Family (Insights and Application Workbook)*. Texas: *Insight For Living*, 2004. Print.

Thoele, Sue Patton. *The Courage to Be Yourself: A Women's Guide to Emotional Strength and Self-Esteem*. Berkeley, CA: Conari, 2001. Print.

Wolraich, Mark L., MD. "Guidance for Effective Discipline." *Pediatrics* 101.4 (April 1, 1998): 723-728. Print.

Van Buren, Abigail. "Quotes." *Hearts & Mind*. n.p., n.d. Web. 22 August 2012.

Endnotes

i. Angelou, Maya. "Mothers: The 5 Questions You Need To Ask Yourself". *The Oprah Magazine.* September 2004.

ii. Neite, Dorothy Law. "Children Learn What They Live". *100 Ways to Enhance Self-Concept in the Classroom: A Handbook for Teachers and Parents.*

iii. Fiese, Barbara H., Thomas J. Tomcho, Michael Douglas, Kimberly Josephs, Scott Poltrock, and Tim Baker. "A Review of 50 Years of Research on Naturally Occurring Family Routines and Rituals: Cause for Celebration?" *Journal of Family Psychology.* 16.4

iv. Thoele, Sue Patton. *The Courage to Be Yourself: A Women's Guide to Emotional Strength and Self-Esteem.*

v. Wolraich, Mark L. MD. "Guidance for Effective Discipline" Pediatrics Vol. 101 No. 4.

vi. Brazleton, T. Berry, and Joshua D. Sparrow. *Discipline: The Brazelton Way.*

vii. Mandela, Nelson. *ThinkExist.com Quotations.*

viii. Friedman, Thomas. "How about Better Parents?" *NY Times Web*.

ix. "Career Center Article." *Berkeley Web*.

x. Swindoll, Charles R. *The Strong Family (Insights and Application Workbook)*

xi. Koch, Wendy. "Record Number of Foster Kids Leave Program as Adults." *USA Today*. 23 May 2007.

xii. "Children of Incarcerated Parents." *Oregon Department of Corrections Web*.

xiii. Gibbs, Nancy. "The Magic of the Family Meal." *Time*. 04 June 2006.

xiv. Van Buren, Abigail. *Hearts & Mind*.

xv. Neirfert, Marianne E. *Dr. Mom's Parenting Guide: Common-Sense Guidance for the Life of your Child*.

xvi. Kahn, Ada P. *Encyclopedia of Mental Health*.

xvii. Fulghum, Robert. *All I Really Need to Know I learned in Kindergarten*.

xviii. "Children of Alcoholics." *American Academy of Child & Adolescent Psychiatry*.

xix. Schwarz, Joel. "Children Whose Parents Smoked Are Twice as Likely to Begin Smoking between 13 and 21." *Medical News Today*. 01 Oct. 2005.

xx. Marston, Stephanie. *The Magic of Encouragement*.

xxi. Josephson, Michael. "The Six Pillars of Character." *Josephson Institute Center for Youth Ethics*.

xxii. Goleman, Daniel. *Social Intelligence: The New Science of Human Relationships.*

xxiii. Novotney, Amy. "Beat the Cheat." *American Psychological Association.*

xxiv. Henderson, Judith. *ThinkExist.com Quotations.*

xxv. Garofalo, Wolf R. "Sexual Orientation and Risk of Suicide Attempts among a Representative Sample of Youth." *Pediatric Adolescent Medicine.*

xxvi. Caruso, Kevin. "Teen Suicide and Youth Suicide." *Suicide Prevention, Suicide Awareness, Suicide Support.*

xxvii. Nelson, Laura J. "Priest Says All Are Welcome in His Church." *The Boston Globe.* 13 June 2011.

xxviii. Doskow, Emily. *Nolo's Essential Guide to Divorce.*

xxix. Neuman, M. Gary., and Patricia Romanowski Bashe. *Helping Your Kids Cope with Divorce the Sandcastles Way.*

xxx. Neuman, M. Gary. "Adult Children of Divorce Confront Parents". *Oprah ABC.*

xxxi. Ginott, Haim. *Between Parent and Child: The Bestselling Classic That Revolutionized Parent-Child Communication.*

xxxii. Morrison, Toni. "Oprah's Most Memorable Guests: the Greatest Lessons on the Oprah Show." *Oprah ABC.*